THE FREE COOKBOOK

On the cover: **Golden Popovers (Yeast Free); Pasta Salad (Gluten Free)**
and Lemon Yogurt Parfait with Berries (Sugar Free)

THE FREE COOKBOOK

Yeast-Free, Gluten-Free, Sugar-Free Secrets to Healthier Living

DIANE BUGEIA AUGUST

Two Harbors Press

Two Harbors Press
212 3rd Avenue North, Suite 290
Minneapolis, MN 55401
612.455.2293
www.TwoHarborsPress.com

ISBN: 978-1-937293-34-5
LCCN: 2011937813

Book sales for North America and international:
Itasca Books, 3501 Highway 100 South, Suite 220
Minneapolis, MN 55416
Phone: 952.345.4488 (toll free 1.800.901.3480)
Fax: 952.920.0541; email: orders@itascabooks.com

Photos: Ron Bez Photography
Book Design by Madge Duffy

Printed in the United States of America

Contents

Dedication

I dedicate this book to Aracely Plateroti, O.M.D., Ph.D, who is the first doctor to ever listen to me and who was therefore able to correctly diagnose my illnesses. Her constant care and attention have made a huge affect on my health and my life! Without her faith and encouragement I would never have imagined writing this book. I can never thank you enough, Aracely—you are truly an angel.

To my dad, Richard A. Bugeia, who encouraged me to cook and always said, "You should try everything at least once." I miss you, Daddy!

And, to my sweet Wally. You are the best boy any mom could ever have! I miss you honey and I'll always love you.

Acknowledgment

I would like to acknowledge John Parks Trowbridge, M.D., and Morton Walker, D.P.M., for writing the book *The Yeast Syndrome*, for it has truly changed my life for the better, and for that and my newly found health I am forever grateful! I have read several other books on the subject of Candida, but none of them had the comprehensive information that their book has. Thanks to these men, others and myself have gotten an answer to our previously undiagnosed ailments and a method for relieving them.

I would especially like to acknowledge and thank Dr. Trowbridge for all of his help and advice in getting this book published. It really made this journey a lot easier.

Disclaimer

This book is not intended to diagnose, treat, or cure any disease. The recipes in this book are based on the diet outlined in the book *The Yeast Syndrome* by John Parks Trowbridge, M.D., and Morton Walker, D.P.M. For more information on Candida and the four-phase CHE (Celebration of Healthy Eating) diet, you should read their book and then consult a licensed health care professional for your treatment to cure Candida.

The author of this book, *The Free Cookbook -- Yeast-Free, Gluten-Free, Sugar-Free Secrets to Healthier Living*, is not a medical doctor or medical practitioner of any sort and has no medical training. You should check with a licensed health care professional before starting or following any diet program.

Introduction

I would like to start by saying that I am not a health care provider of any sort. I developed this cookbook because in 2010, I found out that the minor "disorders" I suffered from were due to a Candida yeast overgrowth. Candida doesn't cause any diseases, but it weakens your immune system to the point where your body is susceptible to disease. The only cure for Candida is a very strict diet, so I came up with great-tasting recipes to make the diet a little easier to follow. I wanted to find a way to share the recipes I created to help others on their journeys through the diet. My hope is that these recipes will not only feed your stomach but also feed your soul!

My search for a diagnosis began four years earlier, when I started seeking out a medical answer for the obesity that had recently plagued me. I had been "chubby" (ten to twenty-five pounds overweight) most of my life, but when I became eighty pounds overweight, I knew that something was physically wrong with me!

I've always eaten healthy. I buy organic food whenever possible. I never eat junk food or fast food, not because of my incredible willpower, but because I don't like the taste of them. I wasn't raised on packaged foods; my mother said it was because we couldn't afford them. Whatever the reason, I'm truly grateful for growing up that way. I've never been a big eater of carbohydrates or sweets, nor do I like soda or coffee. You can imagine my frustration when every western-trained medical doctor, and even some alternative medicine practitioners I went to, looked at me as though I must be lying when they saw me and heard my story.

My luck finally changed when I went to see Aracely Plateroti, O.M.D, Ph.D., at the Plateroti Center in Atascadero, California. She listened to my story and immediately tested me for Candida. Most people think that being tested with a stool sample will determine candida yeast overgrowth. This is not the case, which is why I was diagnosed through bio-energetic medicine, which is vital in evaluating systemic candida. I had heard the name Candida before, but, as I had been told by my previous doctor, I thought it was a catch-all phrase like "autoimmune disorder" has become. I didn't want to hear one more doctor use that term (autoimmune disorder) to classify symptoms that they had no cure for. I don't know why so many doctors are satisfied giving a name to something that they haven't been able to diagnose so they don't feel they have to try to treat it!

As it turns out, she also discovered that my weight problem was not only from the Candida, but from adrenal fatigue and a non-functioning hypothalamus. The Candida did cause many other health problems as well, including sinusitis, extreme sun sensitivity, allergies, sensitive teeth, and a skin rash (one of the typical candida reactions) that had been biopsied three times, by other doctors, but couldn't be diagnosed or cured before.

Once I was diagnosed with Candida, I looked on the Internet for more information. I was rather impressed with some of the information I had acquired, but I wanted to understand it even better.

I was in a health food store when I came across a book entitled *The Yeast Syndrome* by John Parks Trowbridge, M.D., and Morton Walker, D.P.M.. I bought the book and quickly started on my journey to health and wellness.

I will be forever indebted to these doctors for giving me such vital information. I encourage everyone to buy their book and take the questionnaire to see if you too may be suffering from Candida.

I hope that anyone who has been suffering from any of the side effects of Candida finds not only peace of mind but also wellness of body from reading their book. It has literally changed my life for the better, and I hope it does the same for you or someone you love!

How To Use This Book

This book is intended to give anyone who is following a yeast-controlled diet, some easy-to-make and delicious-to-eat recipes.

In order to understand why anyone would need to follow a yeast-controlled diet, I recommend that you read the book *The Yeast Syndrome,* by John Parks Trowbridge, M.D., and Morton Walker, D.P.M.. In their book is a questionnaire that will help you to determine whether you may have Candida and therefore need to find a licensed health care professional that has been trained in curing the disease. Their book will also explain why so many western-trained doctors do not acknowledge Candida as a disease and why they will be unable to treat you for it.

The Yeast Syndrome has an easy to follow four-phase CHE (Celebration of Healthy Eating) diet. All the recipes in my cookbook will reference which of the four phases from their book they are appropriate for.

They will start with the first possible phase, and if the recipe would be better with the addition or substitution of an ingredient that is not allowed until a later phase of the diet, it will be mentioned at the end of the recipe. To know when it's time to move on to the next phase of the diet, you will need to be advised by your health care provider. Since everyone is different, there will be a different timeline for each person to move on to the next phase. Your health care provider may actually have a different yeast-control diet they want you to follow, in which case you'll need to alter the recipes accordingly.

When possible, I made the recipes for just one or two servings so you won't have many leftovers, since even the beginning of spoiled food will increase the Candida. Check all food (veggies, fruits, condiments, and leftovers) for spoilage, and at the first sign, throw them out! When the recipe makes more than one or two servings, I suggest that you freeze the leftovers in single portions for later enjoyment. This is not intended to be a weight loss diet, so portion sizes aren't included in the recipes. Use your judgement to determine the appropriate quantity for yourself.

Keep in mind that all ovens vary, so use the temperatures and cooking times provided as a guide.

All food is best if organic—grown without fertilizers, herbicides, or pesticides—because these chemicals may increase your Candida. If you can't afford or find organic produce, try shopping at the farmers' market in your area. Sometimes the produce has not been grown with fertilizers, herbicides, or pesticides, but the farmer doesn't have the certification to be called Certified Organic. Worst case, you'll be getting the freshest produce (and sometimes meat and seafood as well) available from your local farmers at a great price.

All recipes in this book that call for salt are intended to use kosher salt, which has a lower amount of sodium per measure than iodized salt. If you are using iodized salt, you may want to start with half the amount in the recipe and then adjust to taste. All spices should be ground from the seed or bark whenever possible. See the ground spice recipes under "Condiments" in this book for details. As I mention there, do the best you can with this.

When a recipe calls for rice milk or soy milk, it is always unsweetened and organic. Tofu, as well as any other soy product, if allowed, is also always organic. If soy products are not allowed by your healthcare provider, substitute rice milk in Phase 2, or almond milk in Phase 3.

The butter I use is organic and unsalted. If you are using salted butter, make sure you adjust the salt in the recipe.

When I list oil in a recipe, it is to be whatever oil you wish that is allowed in the phase you're in. If I list olive oil, it's pure olive oil, not extra-virgin (which is stronger in flavor, more expensive, and has a lower smoke point in cooking). When olive oil is used raw, as in salad dressings, pesto, and so on, it should be extra-virgin because the first-pressed strong flavor of this oil is preferable.

The flour you use should be gluten-free, but it doesn't have to be brown rice flour as I state in most of my recipes. I like brown rice flour because it has a nutty flavor and it's really good at giving things that are pan-sautéed a really crisp texture. For making pie dough, I prefer Namaste Foods' Gluten Free Perfect Flour Blend. This makes pie crust flaky and tender, which I haven't found to be the case with brown rice flour—or any other gluten-free flour that I tried, for that matter. Use whatever resources you have and experiment with different (allowed) ingredients to find what works best for you.

I only use xylitol as a sweetener in my recipes. You don't have to use it, but I like it best of all *natural* sugar substitutes (which it must be). The only caution I'd give you if you're trying to convert a favorite recipe of yours from white sugar to xylitol is that, even though it's supposed to be a one-for-one measure for sugar, it can make things sweeter than sugar does, so you may have to adjust the quantity. Some other *natural* sugar substitutes have a bitter aftertaste that I don't like, so this is purely an individual choice.

When using vanilla, it must be pure vanilla extract or fresh vanilla bean (no fake stuff here).

When a recipe calls for berries (or any other fruit for that matter), they are always unsweetened and organic.

While on a Candida diet, you should not use anything artificial, because the chemicals in them may contribute to increasing your Candida. Again, this is something for you and your health care provider to discuss.

Even though the CHE diet says you can have cured, smoked meats like bacon, sausage, ham, corned beef, and pastrami, you need to be sure that they haven't been smoked or cured with any sugar. The nutrition label may say "Sugars: 0", but if you look at the ingredients list, there may be several kinds of sugar that were used to smoke or cure the meat. *Read ingredient labels carefully!*

While you're on the strict phases of a Candida diet, you can't have any vinegars or fermented products. This includes mayonnaise, mustard, horseradish sauce, chili sauce, soy sauce, and so on. This is why I have listed so many condiments in my book.

When an ingredient has an asterisk (*) in front of it, it means that there's a recipe for that ingredient elsewhere in this book. I know this can seem cumbersome, but you need to avoid additives such as citric acid during the first three phases of the diet. Most canned and a lot of frozen foods, like whole peeled tomatoes, tomato sauce, tomato paste, artichoke hearts, and green chilies, have added citric acid. Again, read labels carefully!

There are recipes where I recommend special equipment. The equipment is usually not absolutely necessary but is generally inexpensive, will make the recipe easier to follow, and is worth the investment, in my opinion.

I encourage everyone to use these recipes as a guideline and to make changes that suit your palate. Be creative and have fun making them your own.

Condiments

AP (All-Purpose) Seasoning (Phase 1)

I use this for everything from meats, fish, and eggs to soups and sauces.
Change the ingredients to make this to your own taste.

3 tbsp. sweet paprika
2 tbsp. salt
2 tbsp. garlic powder
2 tbsp. onion powder
1½ tbsp. dried marjoram (or you may substitute with 1 tbsp. oregano)
1 tbsp. dried thyme
1 tbsp. pepper

Combine all ingredients and store in an airtight container.

Taco Seasoning (Phase 2)

2 tbsp. chili powder

2 tbsp. ground cumin seeds

2 tbsp. salt

1 tbsp. paprika

$\frac{1}{8}$ tsp. pepper

1 tbsp. onion powder

1 tbsp. garlic powder

$\frac{1}{8}$ tsp. cayenne (optional)

Combine all ingredients well and store in an airtight container.

Celery Salt (Phase 1)

To make celery salt, grind celery seeds and mix with an equal amount of salt. Store in an airtight container.

Ground Spices; Garlic and Onion Powders (Phase 1)

I suggest that you grind whole spices rather than use the commercial ones whenever possible. The commercial ones contain stabilizers along with the spice that you're expecting. The stabilizers are necessary to keep the spices running through the equipment at the spice factories, but they are not preferable while on this diet (do the best you can here).

It's simple to buy bulk dehydrated onions and garlic, as well as seeds or whole spices, for most of your other spice needs (this includes but is not limited to cumin seeds, mustard seeds, and celery seeds) in bulk, at the health food store and grind them up yourself in a spice grinder. You can buy a coffee/spice grinder for under $15 and use it for grinding spices only. You don't want to use it to grind coffee too, or the coffee will taste like spices.

Store the spices in an airtight container. I like to wash out and reuse empty herb and spice jars and put new labels on them.

Berry Syrup (Phase 3)
(Pictured on Crepes)

2 cups unsweetened berries of your choice

1–2 tbsp. xylitol (depending on the sweetness of the berries)

1 tsp. lemon juice

¼ cup water

Heat all ingredients to a boil on medium-high heat for 10–15 minutes. Reduce heat to low and simmer for 15–20 minutes (stirring occasionally) until fruit has broken down and mixture has thickened to a syrupy consistency (you may mash with a potato masher or fork if you'd like). Store in an airtight container in the refrigerator.

Berry Jam (Phase 3)
(Pictured on Cover with Popover)

2 cups berries of your choice

2 – 3 tsp. xylitol

$\frac{1}{8}$ tsp. pure vanilla extract

$\frac{1}{8}$ tsp. cinnamon (optional)

1 pinch of salt

$\frac{1}{4}$ cup water

$\frac{1}{4}$ tsp. lemon juice

Place all ingredients in a small saucepan and bring to a boil. Reduce heat to a simmer and cook for 30-40 minutes, stirring occasionally until thickened. Place in an airtight container and store in the refrigerator or freeze for use later.

Cranberry Sauce (Phase 3)

1 cup water
¾ cup xylitol
12 oz. fresh or frozen cranberries
zest of ½ lemon

Bring water and xylitol to a boil. Add cranberries and lemon zest, and return to a boil. Cook, stirring occasionally, until all the cranberries have popped. Remove from heat to cool completely. Refrigerate for at least two hours before serving. Store in an airtight container for later use.

Tip: For even more flavor, you can add a cinnamon stick when you add the cranberries. Remove the cinnamon stick before cooling.

Tzatziki Sauce (Phase 1)

(Pictured on Falafel Salad)

½ cup cucumber — seeds removed, thinly sliced

1 tsp + ½ tsp. salt

1 cup Greek yogurt

2 tsp. fresh mint — chopped

½ tsp. oregano

1 clove garlic — chopped

Place the cucumber in a sieve or small colander and sprinkle with 1 teaspoon of salt. Work the salt into the cucumber and let sit for 30 minutes. Rinse the salt off of the cucumber and press out all the water. Blot the cucumber dry and place in a blender or small food processor. Add all the other ingredients to the cucumber and blend. Refrigerate for at least 2 hours (preferably overnight) before using for the most flavor.

Tip: You may use this as a dipping sauce for *falafels or any meat kabobs.

Tip 2: For thicker sauce, if using regular yogurt, place the yogurt in a sieve, lined with a coffee filter, and suspended over a bowl in the refrigerator overnight. Discard the liquid and continue the recipe as above.

Phase 2: Add ½ teaspoon olive oil.

Phase 3: Add ½ teaspoon lemon juice.

Compound Butter (Phase 1)

Make sure you experiment with the ingredients and make it to your taste.

1 cube of butter — softened
½ tsp. salt
2 tbsp. chives — finely chopped
¼ tsp. *AP seasoning
1 tbsp. parsley — finely chopped
½ tsp. basil — finely chopped
¼ tsp. garlic — minced or pressed

Mix all ingredients thoroughly, and either place in an airtight container and keep refrigerated for 4 hours before using, or place in plastic wrap and form into a 1" log shape and place in the freezer for at least 2 hours before using. When ready to use, you may slice ½" off of the log and place on a cooked steak, fish fillet, piece of chicken, or any vegetables you like.

Tip: Don't limit yourself to savory compound butters. Try berries mixed with butter, cinnamon a pinch of salt and xylitol for an addition to *crepes or in Phase 4 with just about anything!

Phase 2: Add ⅛ tsp. cayenne pepper (optional)

Phase 3: Add lemon or lime zest and/or a little citrus juice (optional).

Corn Tortillas (Phase 3)

2 cups masa

1¼ cups water

¼ tsp. salt

Mix the masa, water, and salt for 2 minutes to form a soft dough. If the dough is dry, add extra water (1 teaspoon at a time) until it reaches the desired texture.

Place thick pieces of plastic cut to fit on each side of a tortilla press (I recommend cutting up a gallon-size plastic storage bag), or you can form these by hand if you're able.

Divide dough into 10–12 equal-sized balls and press between the plastic-lined tortilla press.

Heat a nonstick skillet or comal (a Mexican pan for cooking tortillas) on medium-high to high. Cook each tortilla for 2–5 minutes per side until blistered and lightly browned.

Tip: You can find tortilla presses at most Mexican markets for under $20.

Tip 2: If not using right away, place in a zip-top bag in the refrigerator or in the freezer for longer storage.

Mock Tortillas (Phase 1)

1 large egg
$\frac{1}{8}$ tsp. *AP seasoning
$\frac{1}{2}$ tsp. butter or oil

Mix the egg and seasoning in a small blender or food processor. Heat fat in a 10" pan and add the egg mixture. Roll the pan around to make an even, thin coating in the pan.

Heat for about one minute or until egg mixture is set and pulling away from the edges of the pan. Carefully flip over and cook an additional 30 seconds and remove from pan (you may need to coax it out of the pan with a spatula).

You can use these with your favorite fillings for any savory application.

Note: You can replace the *AP seasoning with the same amount of salt for a different savory version or a little salt and xilitol for a sweet version if you'd like.

Note 2: This will yield one large mock tortilla.

Fresh Horseradish (Phase 1)

1" length of fresh horseradish — peeled and finely grated (I use a microplane for this).

Store in an airtight container in the refrigerator for future use.

Horseradish Sauce (Phase 1)

2 tbsp. grated horseradish (prepared as above)
1 tbsp. *mayonnaise (Phase 1) or Greek yogurt

Mix the horseradish and *mayonnaise or yogurt together well and store in an airtight container in the refrigerator for a few days, or use immediately.

Tip: Use the horseradish prepared either way as a condiment for steaks, roast beef, pork, and other hearty meats and poultry.

Tartar Sauce (Phase 1)

½ cup *mayonnaise (Phase 1)

¼ cup plain Greek yogurt

¾ tsp. dill weed

¾ tsp. *celery salt

¼ cup cucumber — finely minced

Mix all ingredients well. Store in an airtight container in the refrigerator for up to a few days.

This is best if it sits in the refrigerator for several hours or overnight.

Phase 2: Add 1 – 2 tsp. finely minced capers (packed in salt only!), rinsed. Do not substitute with brined capers as they contain vinegar.

Phase 3: Add 1 tsp. fresh lemon juice (and lemon zest if desired).

Italian-Style Dressing (Phase 1)

1 large clove garlic — peeled and roughly chopped

1½ tbsp. *AP seasoning

⅔ cup oil

½ cup water

3 – 4 anchovy fillets or 2 tsp. anchovy paste

½ tsp. salt

½ tsp. pepper

Place all ingredients in a blender or mini food processor and blend thoroughly. The texture will be thinner than regular Italian dressing, but the flavor will be very similar.

Store in an airtight container in the refrigerator.

To make a creamy version, simply add ⅓ cup *mayonnaise and ½ cup plain yogurt and omit the water and oil.

Phase 2: You may add 2 tsp. rinsed capers (packed in salt only, not brined) for more flavor.

Phase 3: You may add 2 tsp. lemon juice.

Phase 4: Replace water with 2 tbsp. red wine vinegar; increase oil to ¾ cup; reduce the *AP seasoning to 2 tsp.

Caesar-Style Dressing (Phase 3)

¾ cup extra-virgin olive oil

4 whole anchovy filets (or 1 tbsp. anchovy paste)

¼ cup Parmesan cheese

2 tbsp. lemon juice

1 egg (coddled if pregnant, nursing, or elderly, or you may buy pasteurized eggs)

1 large clove garlic — peeled and roughly chopped

1 tsp. ground mustard seeds

½ tsp. salt

⅛ tsp. pepper

Combine all ingredients in a blender or small food processor and blend thoroughly. Store in an airtight container in the refrigerator.

Mayonnaise (Phase 1)

I have included some very uncustomary ingredients here because otherwise I find it to be very bland in flavor. Please experiment with this to find the right balance of flavor for you.

¼ + 1 cup oil
1 whole egg
¼ tsp. salt
¼ tsp. *celery salt
⅛ tsp. onion powder
pinch of xylitol
1 tsp. anchovy paste (optional, but I highly recommend it)

In a food processor, pour in the ¼ cup oil, egg, salt, *celery salt, onion powder, xylitol, and anchovy paste. Let run on high until yolks become light in color and mixture has thickened (about 1–2 minutes). In a *very* slow dribble, pour the 1 cup of oil through the feed tube increasing to a very slow, steady stream as the mixture thickens to a solid (you'll be able to see and hear it slap against the inside of the food processor bowl as it becomes solid). You may need to stop and scrape down the sides and then restart the food processor to continue. Once all the oil is in and the mixture is thickened, place it in an airtight container in the refrigerator.

Note: Since this doesn't have the preservatives that commercial mayonnaise does, you'll need to use it in a matter of days, not weeks or months!

Phase 2: You can add ½ tsp. ground yellow mustard seed in the beginning, with the other seasonings, to improve the flavor.

Phase 3: After adding only half of the 1 cup of oil, you may add ½ tsp. lemon juice, then continue with the remaining ½ cup of oil as above.

Cocktail Sauce (Phase 1)

¼ cup celery — finely minced
1 cup *tomato sauce
¼ cup fresh horseradish — grated
¼ tsp. salt
⅛ tsp. pepper

Mix all ingredients, cover, and refrigerate until thoroughly chilled.

Phase 2: Add a pinch of cayenne (or more, if you like it really hot).

Phase 3: Add ½ tablespoon lemon juice.

Phase 4: Replace the cayenne with ⅛ teaspoon hot pepper sauce if you prefer.

Ranch-Style Dressing (Phase 1)

1 cup *mayonnaise

1 cup Greek yogurt

1 tsp. dried basil

1 tsp. dried oregano

1 tsp. dried thyme

½ tsp. salt (+ more to taste)

½ tsp. onion powder

½ tsp. garlic powder

¼ tsp. *celery salt

⅛ tsp. pepper (+ more to taste)

1 tbsp. water (if needed for desired thickness)

Mix all ingredients in a blender or food processor. Adjust water, salt, and pepper to taste.

Note: If you use fresh onion it will increase the liquid content, making the dressing runny and increasing the sharpness of the onion flavor.

If you use green onion or chives, they will turn the dressing green. This will not hurt the flavor, but if you want white ranch-style dressing, you need to use white or yellow onion or onion powder.

Onion Dip (Phase 1)

¹/₂ cup Greek yogurt
¹/₂ cup *mayonnaise (Phase 1)
1 tsp. onion powder
1 tsp. dehydrated onion
¹/₈ tsp. salt

Mix all ingredients and let sit covered in the refrigerator for several hours or overnight. This will allow the ingredients to completely combine for the best flavor.

Serve with *crudités platter for variety from *ranch-style dressing.

Garlic Aioli (Phase 2)

(Pictured with Crab Cakes)

½ cup *mayonnaise
1 large clove garlic — minced or pressed
⅛ tsp. *AP Seasoning

Blend all ingredients in a small blender or food processor until smooth and creamy. Refrigerate in an airtight container until ready to use.

Tip: This is a great condiment to *crab cakes.

Sliced Almond Snacks (Phase 3)

1 cup sliced almonds
2 tsp. olive oil
2 tbsp. *AP seasoning

Preheat oven to 325°. Place all ingredients on a sheet pan and toss to combine. Try to get an even coating of seasoning on the almonds, then spread them on the sheet pan in a single layer.

Bake for 10 minutes, then cool. Place in an airtight container or zip-top bag.

Tip: Besides snacking on these, you can use them to top salads or soups in place of croutons. Or you can grind them up and use them as a coating for meat or fish.

Tip 2: Use the same steps with any other nut or seasoning conbinations you like!

Special Applesauce (Phase 3)

6 tart apples (such as Granny Smith) — diced into about 1" pieces

1 tsp. xylitol

1 tsp. fresh lemon juice

½ tsp. cinnamon

pinch of salt

¼ tsp. vanilla

½ cup water

Bring all ingredients to a boil, then reduce heat to simmer. Let simmer for 20–30 minutes until apples become very soft.

Mash with a fork or potato masher until the consistency of applesauce.

Chill for at least 1 hour.

This is a great accompaniment to *pork loin roulade and *pork chops and scalloped potatoes.

Tip: For a pure applesauce without the extra flavoring, you can follow the directions above but only use the apples and water.

Tip 2: If using sweet apples, omit the xylitol.

Tomato Salsa (Phase 1)

(Pictured over Chicken Enchiladas)

This is great on scrambled eggs with a dollop of plain yogurt and a sprinkle of chives, on a piece of grilled fish, or with fajitas!

1½ Lb. *whole peeled tomatoes — roughly chopped

½ jalapeño pepper — roughly chopped (seeds and ribs removed)

½ green bell pepper — roughly chopped

¼ cup red onion — roughly chopped

1 tsp. salt

½ tsp. pepper

1 green onion — sliced (green and white parts)

2 tbsp. fresh cilantro — roughly chopped

1 large clove garlic — roughly chopped

Combine all ingredients in a blender or food processor. If you like it chunky, pulse rather than blend it until it reaches the desired texture. This will taste best if it sits overnight.

Phase 3: Add 1 tbsp. lime juice.

Phase 4: Reduce lime juice to ½ teaspoon and add 1 teaspoon red wine vinegar

Whole Peeled Tomatoes (Phase 1)

Quantity is not important in this recipe, but keep in mind they won't last as long in the refrigerator as canned ones do, so try to only make as many as you will use in a couple of days.

2 Lb. fresh tomatoes

Bring a large pot of water to a boil. Have a large bowl of ice water on the side. In the meantime, cut the cores out of the tomatoes and slice an "X" on the bottom of each tomato. Dip the tomatoes into the boiling water for 30–60 seconds, then immediately plunge them into the ice water. Let cool in the ice water for about one minute, then slip the skins off, discard them, and reserve the peeled tomatoes in an airtight container. Add ½ teaspoon salt per pint of tomatoes (optional) and refrigerate, or use right away.

Roasted Green Chilies (Phase 2)

2 whole Anaheim or Poblano chilies

Place peppers on a grill, under a broiler, or on a gas burner. Let the skins get completely black and blistered on all sides.

Remove to a paper bag (closed up) or to a bowl covered with plastic wrap so the skins steam off of the peppers. Let cool for 15–20 minutes, then pull the skins off and remove the seeds. Now the peppers are ready for use.

Tomato Sauce (Phase 1)

$\frac{1}{3}$ cup onion-chopped

$\frac{1}{2}$ bell pepper chopped

4 large or 6 medium *whole peeled tomatoes (about 1$\frac{1}{2}$ – 2 Lb.)-chopped

1 large clove garlic-smashed or roughly chopped

1$\frac{1}{2}$ tbsp. oil

1 tsp. basil

1 tsp. thyme

$\frac{1}{2}$ tsp. oregano

$\frac{1}{2}$ tsp. *AP seasoning

$\frac{1}{2}$ tsp. salt

$\frac{1}{4}$ tsp. pepper

Sauté onion and bell pepper in a saucepan until onion is translucent (about 3-5 minutes). Add remaining ingredients and stir to combine. Press the large tomato chunks with the back of a fork or with a potato masher to break them up.

Bring to a boil, then cover and reduce heat to low. Simmer for 45-50 minutes.

Allow mixture to cool before blending. Put all ingredients into a blender or food processor and blend until completely smooth.

Store in an airtight container in the refrigerator or use right away.

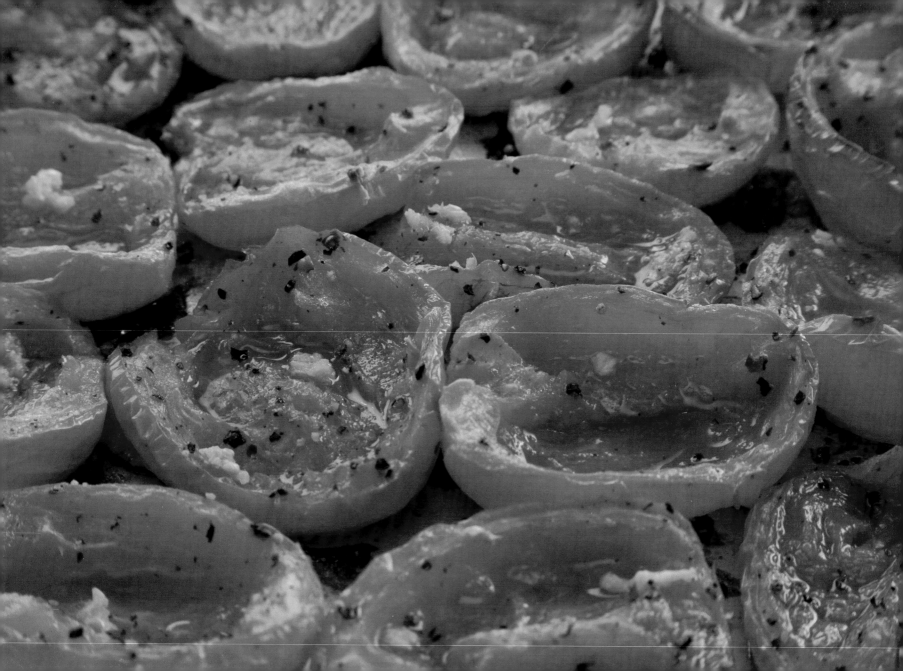

Tomato Paste (Phase 1)

(Pictured on Opposite Page)

4 Roma (or plum) tomatoes — sliced lengthwise, cores and seeds removed
½ tsp. oil
1 small garlic clove — finely minced or pressed (optional)
½ tsp. salt
⅛ tsp. pepper

Preheat oven to 450°. Place the tomato halves, cut side up, on a sheet pan and toss with the oil, garlic, salt, and pepper. If the tomatoes are small, you may only need to roast them for 40–50 minutes. If the tomatoes are large, they could take an hour to an hour and a half. The tomatoes should have very little moisture left in them. Once roasted, slip off the skins and discard.
Place tomatoes in a mini food processor and process until the consistency of tomato paste.

Tip: The quantity you make of this is not important. You may double or triple this recipe and use it right away, or keep it in the freezer in tablespoon-sized blobs (for easy portioning) to use later.

White Sauce (Phase 2)

2 tbsp. butter
2 tbsp. brown rice flour
1 cup soy milk
½ tsp. salt
⅛ tsp. pepper

Melt butter, over medium-high heat, whisk in seasoning and flour; continue to whisk and cook for 1–2 minutes. Add the milk all at once and whisk until thickened. You may add other seasonings to this if you'd like.

Tip: You may substitute the salt and pepper for ¾ tsp. *AP seasoning for more flavor.

Cheese Sauce (Phase 2)

Make the *white sauce above, and at the end add ¼ – ⅓ cup of shredded Colby or Jack cheese and stir until it's melted.

Tip: Enjoy this on veggies or mixed with cooked brown rice pasta for "mac & cheese".

Phase 3 & 4: Substitute with any allowed cheese.

Pesto Sauce (Phase 2)

Zest of ½ lemon

2 tsp. lemon juice

3 garlic cloves — peeled and roughly chopped

¾ cup pine nuts — toasted

2 cups basil leaves

1– 2 anchovy filets or 1 tsp. anchovy paste (optional)

½ cup Parmesan cheese

⅔ cup extra-virgin olive oil

Place all ingredients, except the oil, in a food processor and turn on high. While processor is running, slowly drizzle in the oil. When all the oil is incorporated, turn off the processor and scrape down the sides.

You may either use it right away or store it in an airtight container in the refrigerator.

Tip: You may substitute spinach or arugula for the basil to create a different flavor of pesto.

Tip 2: If you're going to keep this in the refrigerator for more than a day or two, pour a thin layer of extra virgin olive oil on top of it so as to keep the green color and freshness longer.

Appetizers

Cocktail Meatballs (Phase 1)

1 tbsp. oil
1 recipe *meatloaf-uncooked mixture

Preheat oven to 400°. Form meat into 1–1½" balls. Place meatballs on a rack on top of a sheet pan and bake for 15 minutes or until brown. You may turn them over halfway through cooking for more even browning, but they will be fully cooked either way.

Present with toothpicks on the side for easy serving.

Tip: Put the cooked meatballs in a slow cooker on low and cover with 1½–cups *chicken stock. This will keep them warm throughout the party and add even more moisture and flavor!

Tip 2: You may freeze these after baking, then put them in a slow cooker (as stated above) for about 30 minutes or until heated through.

Artichoke & Spinach Dip

2 bags triple-washed spinach (12-14 oz. fresh, well-washed bunches of spinach)

1 tsp. salt

1 tbsp. olive oil

1 cup onion-finely minced

3 large cloves garlic-minced or pressed

16 oz. cream cheese-room temperature

2 tbsp. lemon juice

2 tsp. mustard powder

½ tsp. dried basil

⅛ tsp. nutmeg

2 anchovy filets or 1 tsp. anchovy paste

4 fresh artichoke hearts-steamed or boiled for 12-15 minutes, then chopped to ¼-½" dice

1 cup jack cheese-shredded

⅓ + ⅓ cup Parmesan cheese-grated

2 egg yolks

1 tsp. *AP seasoning

1 tbsp. butter (to butter the baking dish)

Roughly chop spinach and sauté with onion and garlic in oil for 3-5 minutes until softened. Cover and refrigerate until cool.

Preheat oven to 350°. Beat the cream cheese, lemon juice, mustard powder, basil, nutmeg and anchovy until smooth (you may use an electric mixer if you'd like). Stir in the spinach, artichoke hearts, jack cheese, ⅓ cup Parmesan, egg yolks, and *AP seasoning, mixing well to combine.

Butter a 2-quart casserole dish and pour in the mixture. Sprinkle the other ⅓ cup Parmesan on top and bake for 30 minutes or until brown and bubbly.

Tip: Serve with *crudités platter for a warm dip option.

Tip 2: Add salad shrimp or crab for a heartier version.

Potato Bites (Phase 2)

2–3 lb. small boiling potatoes

3 tbsp. Greek yogurt

3 tbsp. caviar (make sure you don't use a metal spoon or it will taint the caviar!)

3 tbsp. chives — finely chopped (optional)

Boil potatoes whole in salted water until fork-tender. Cool completely before cutting open (this will ensure they keep their shape).

Cut chilled potatoes in half and top each cut side with a small dollop of yogurt, ¼ tsp. of caviar, and a sprinkling of chives (optional).

These make beautiful and elegant appetizers!

Tip: Try using some different fish roe in other colors (like bright orange) for a festive platter.

Crudités Platter (Phase 1)

This will make a large platter of crudités for a party. Feel free to cut down the quantity to fit your needs.

1 package baby carrots (or you may cut large carrots into sticks).
4 – 6 celery stalks — cut into 3" x ½" sticks
¼ – ½ head cauliflower — cut into small florets
¼ – ½ head broccoli — cut into small florets
1 pint cherry tomatoes
2 medium zucchini — cut into 3" x ½" sticks
1 cucumber — cut into 3" x ½" sticks
1 cup *ranch-style dressing (or dressing of your choice for phase 1)

Place all veggies on a platter grouped by vegetable. Try to break up the same-colored veggies with different colored veggies in between to add more interest. Put a bowl of *Ranch Style Dressing in the center of the platter or off to one side for easy dipping.

Phase 2: **Add a Phase 2 dressing for dipping.**

Phase 3: **Add a Phase 3 dressing for dipping.**

Crab Cakes (Phase 2)

(Pictured on Opposite Page)

You can serve these with *tarter sauce or *garlic aioli on the side!

2 tbsp. *mayonnaise

¼ tsp. pepper

½ tsp. *AP seasoning

¼ tsp. onion powder

⅛ tsp. garlic powder

4 tsp. green onion-minced

2 tbsp. parsley-minced

¼ cup bell pepper-minced

⅓ cup cooked brown rice

2 eggs

½ Lb. crabmeat-squeezed dry (See tip below)

½ cup brown rice flour

1 tsp. + 2–3 tbsp. olive oil

Stir together the *mayonnaise and seasonings in a bowl and set aside.

Sauté the green onion and bell pepper in the 1 tsp. of oil for 3 minutes. Remove from the pan, let cool, then add to the bowl.

Add the brown rice, eggs, and crab to the bowl and stir to combine.

Divide the mixture into four balls, press into flat cakes, and refrigerate for 1–2 hours.

Spread flour on a dinner plate and lightly press both sides of each cake into the flour. Pat off excess flour so that there's only a light coating of flour on each one.

Heat 1 tbsp. oil on medium-high heat and cook for 3–5 minutes on each side until crisp and golden. Serve with *tarter sauce on the side.

Tip: If using fresh or previously frozen crab, put in double-thickness paper towels and squeeze out the excess liquid. If using canned, press the lid against the crab to squeeze out the liquid then put in double-thickness paper towels and squeeze out any additional liquid. This step is important or the cakes will never hold together.

Tip 2: This makes a great lunch when paired with *coleslaw, *green shrimp salad, *Caesar salad, or *black bean salad.

Tip 3: You can make these smaller and serve them as an appetizer!

Phase 3: Serve with lemon wedges and *garlic aioli or *tarter sauce on the side.

Cucumber Slice Bites (Phase 1)

1 seedless cucumber or zucchini

Pull the tongs of a fork down the length of the cucumber or zucchini on all sides to make grooves in the skin for visual appeal (optional). Cut into ½" slices and top with any spread or topping you like. See suggestions below:

*Chicken salad; egg salad; *creamy crab, shrimp or tuna salad; a dollop of *ranch-style dressing or *onion dip, topped with a cherry tomato (held on with a toothpick through it); or small pieces of *roasted turkey breast, *mock beer can chicken, cooked beef, or shrimp.

Phase 2: Top it with a cube of Phase-2 cheese or cream cheese mixed with *AP seasoning.

Phase 3: Top it with a cube of Phase-3 cheese.

Tip: You may also use thin (¼"-thick) slices of carrot, turnip, radish, or 1½" squares of bell pepper, celeriac, fennel, jicama, or any firm lettuce as a base instead of the cucumber for even more variety and visual interest.

Falafels (Phase 3)

(Pictured on Opposite Page as a Falafel Salad)

1 tbsp. + 1 – 3 tbsp. olive oil

¾ cup onion-chopped

2 large cloves garlic-chopped

1 cup dry garbanzo beans (chickpeas)-soaked in water overnight and drained

1 egg-lightly beaten

½ tsp. salt

¼ tsp. pepper

2 tbsp. brown rice flour

½ cup cooked brown rice

Mix all ingredients except the 1-3 tbsp. of oil in a food processor. You'll need to stop and scrape down the sides a few times until mixture is very smooth (about 5 minutes).

Heat 1 tbsp. of oil on medium-high heat. Spoon mixture by tablespoon into the hot oil and sauté for about 5 minutes per side until well browned and firm to the touch. Add more oil (1 tbsp. at a time) as needed until all of the mixture is cooked.

Drain on paper towels or a brown paper bag and serve with *tzatziki sauce.

Tip: For a tasty lunch, serve 5-7 falafel pieces on a bed of shredded cabbage with *tzatziki sauce drizzled over the top as the dressing.

Turkey or Roast Beef Lettuce Rolls (Phase 1)

4 lettuce leaves (red leaf lettuce or other soft-leaf lettuces work really well)
½ Lb. homemade turkey or roast beef — thinly sliced
1 tbsp. *mayonnaise (Phase 1) or plain yogurt
½ tsp. *AP seasoning
1 tomato — thinly sliced

Lay cleaned and dried lettuce leaves out flat. Spread a thin layer of the *mayonnaise or yogurt on the center of the lettuce leaf. Lightly sprinkle with the *AP seasoning, 1-2 slices of the tomato and 1-2 slices of the meat. Roll into a log shape and secure with toothpicks every 3 inches. Slice logs between toothpicks and serve on a platter as appetizers.

Tip: If you leave the logs whole, they make a good lunch alternative to a sandwich. In addition to the meat above, you can fill them with *chicken salad, or *creamy crab, shrimp, or tuna salad.

Phase 2: Add chopped or thinly sliced avocado for even more flavor, color and texture.

Brunch Dishes

Crepes (Phase 2)

(Pictured on Opposite Page)

1 cup soy milk or rice milk

¾ cup brown rice flour

2 eggs

½ tsp. salt

1 tbsp. melted butter + more for greasing the pan

Mix all ingredients well and let sit (refrigerated) for at least 20 minutes, up to 8 hours. Heat a 6" crepe or omelet pan over medium heat with a light coating of butter (wipe out the excess). Add enough batter to just coat the bottom of the pan, swirling the batter around to coat evenly. Allow the crepe to lightly brown on the first side (about 3 minutes). Flip over and cook the other side for another 1-2 minutes.

Remove from pan and serve filled with chicken (or other meat) and cheese and top with a seasoned *white sauce, if you like.

The possibilities are endless, so let your imagination run wild!

Phase 3: You may add the zest from half of a lemon, 1 teaspoon pure vanilla extract and 1 tablespoon of xylitol to the batter for sweet crepes. You may fill these with berries and *berry syrup on top, if you like.

Frittata (Phase 1)

(Pictured on Opposite Page)

This is one of those recipes that you can add anything you want to it that's in the phase you're in. Be creative and make it your own!

½ Lb. *homemade sausage (or left over *mock beer can chicken-sautéing the chicken is not necessary)

1½ tbsp. oil

½ onion — chopped

1 bell pepper — chopped

1 large clove garlic — minced or pressed

8 eggs

⅓ cup water

2 tsp. *AP seasoning

1 tsp. salt

½ tsp. pepper

1 tsp. thyme

Preheat oven to 400°. Heat an 11-12" pan on medium-high and sauté the *homemade sausage until cooked through, and drain off excess fat. Add the oil, onion, bell pepper, and garlic and sauté until veggies are crisp-tender (about 5 minutes).

Beat eggs, water, *AP seasoning, salt, pepper, and thyme until well combined.

Reduce heat to medium. Pour egg mixture over all. Stir pan to evenly distribute all ingredients and let cook, untouched, for 8 minutes or until the edges start to set.

Place the pan in the oven until it is puffed up and the top is lightly browned (about 4–5 minutes).

Phase 2: Add ½ – ⅔ cup of shredded Colby or Jack cheese with the egg mixture.

Potato Strata (Phase 2)

1 tbsp. butter

½ cup potatoes — thinly sliced (or you may substitute with ⅓ cup cooked brown rice)

½ cup cooked broccoli

1 cup *homemade sausage or cooked chicken

⅓ cup onion or green onion — finely chopped

1½ cups Colby cheese — shredded

4 large eggs

¾ cup rice milk

1 tsp. *AP seasoning

¼ tsp. pepper

Preheat oven to 350°. Butter an 8" x 8" baking dish. Layer the potatoes, broccoli, meat, onion, and half of the cheese in the dish.

In a bowl, whisk the eggs, rice milk, *AP seasoning, and pepper and pour into the casserole dish over the other ingredients. Sprinkle the remaining cheese on top and bake for 40 – 50 minutes or until puffed and golden.

Tip: You can assemble, cover, and refrigerate (uncooked) 8 hours in advance.

Tip 2: You can change out the meat, cheese, and veggies to anything you want that's allowed on the phase you're in.

Chicken and Green Chili, Cheese Soufflé (Phase 2)

2 tbsp. butter (plus more for prepping soufflé dishes)

2 tbsp. brown rice flour (plus more for inside the soufflé dishes)

1 cup soy milk

¾ tsp. salt

⅛ tsp. nutmeg

¼ tsp. pepper

3 egg yolks-beaten

½ cup Colby cheese-grated

½ cup cooked chicken-diced

1 tbsp. cilantro-finely minced

1 green onion-finely sliced (white and green parts)

¼ cup *roasted green chilies-chopped

½ tsp. *AP seasoning

4 egg whites (whites only, no yolk or any other fat in the bowl or they won't whip properly)

Preheat oven to 350°. Melt the 2 tbsp. butter in a saucepan, whisk in flour, and bring to a boil (whisk 1-2 minutes). Add the soy milk all at once (whisking constantly until completely blended), then whisk in the salt, nutmeg, and pepper. Turn off the heat and quickly whisk in the egg yolks so they don't scramble. Add the cheese, chicken, cilantro, onion, *roasted green chilies, *AP seasoning, and corn. Remove to a bowl.

In a separate *very clean bowl with very clean beaters*, beat the egg whites until stiff but not dry. Fold egg whites into the reserved mixture, being careful not to deflate the airiness of the egg whites.

Prepare the soufflé dishes (one 7-inch dish or four 4-ounce dishes) by lightly coating the inside of the dishes with butter and flour (tap out any excess flour).

Spoon mixture into dishes and bake for about 40 minutes or until puffed and firm.

Tip: You may freeze the individual soufflés and bake them later @ 350° for 45–55 minutes or until puffed and firm.

Phase 3: Replace the Colby cheese with cheddar cheese, add ½ cup corn kernels and replace the flour for dusting the soufflé dish with Parmesan cheese for more flavor.

Scrambled Eggs (Phase 1)

(Pictured on Opposite Page with Meat Sauce for Pasta)

2 eggs
2 tsp. butter
Salt and pepper to taste
1 tbsp. water

Whisk eggs, water, salt, and pepper until the whites have combined with the yolks. Melt the butter in a small pan on medium-low and add the eggs to the pan. Wait for about 1 minute, and, using a silicone spatula, gently stir the eggs. I like to move the spatula under the eggs all the way around the pan and underneath the eggs in the bottom/center of the pan. Wait another 30–45 seconds and repeat. This will create fluffy curds instead of dry, crumbly eggs.

Remove eggs while still moist to prevent overcooking and to give you silky, custard-like eggs.

Tip: You may replace the salt and pepper with *AP seasoning for more flavor.

Phase 2: Sprinkle the top of the cooked eggs with any of the cheeses allowed in this phase if you'd like.

Homemade Breakfast Sausage (Phase 1)

⅛ tsp. whole nutmeg — ground

⅛ tsp. ground or whole caraway seeds (optional)

¼ tsp. dried sage

¼ tsp. dried basil

¼ tsp. dried summer savory

1 tsp. *AP seasoning

2 tsp. salt

½ tsp. pepper

¾ Lb. ground pork

Mix all ingredients in a bowl. Cover and let sit overnight in the refrigerator.

Shape into small balls (about golf ball-sized), press into patties, and cook on medium-high heat until juices push up to the top on the first side (about 5-7 minutes). Flip over and cook an additional 5-7 minutes on the second side.

Drain on a brown paper bag or paper towels to remove excess fat.

Tip: To check the seasoning before cooking the whole batch, make a tiny patty and cook it. If you like it, continue; if not, adjust the seasoning to your taste, then continue making the rest of the patties.

Tip 2: You can eat these as breakfast sausage patties or you may crumble the meat and brown it as you would ground beef to put in *meat sauce for pasta, either added to the beef or as a purely sausage meat sauce for pasta.

Steak and Eggs (Phase 1)

You may use leftover steak or breakfast steak instead of cube steak here (see tip below).

For the Eggs:
1½ tsp. butter
1-2 eggs
¼ tsp. salt
⅛ tsp. pepper

Melt the 1½ tsp. butter on medium-low heat and add the egg(s), salt, and pepper. Cook for about 1½ minutes on the first side and about 1 minute on the second side (for over-easy eggs), or until the whites are completely opaque. Remove from the pan and set aside. Feel free to make the eggs any way you may prefer.

For the Steak:
3-4 oz. cube steak-pounded to tenderize
2 tsp. butter or oil
¼ tsp. *AP seasoning

Season the breakfast steak with the *AP seasoning on both sides. In the same pan that you cooked the egg(s), heat the 2 tsp. butter or oil on medium-high. Add the steak and cook the first side until the meat juices push their way to the top side of the steak. Turn and continue to cook for an additional 3–5 minutes or until brown on the bottom. Top with the cooked egg(s) and enjoy!

Tip: If you're using leftover steak instead of the breakfast steak, simply heat it through in the pan (without the addition of oil) after you've cooked the egg(s).

Salads

Chicken Salad (Phase 1)

After I've made a *mock beer can chicken I always have leftovers, and *chicken salad is one of my favorite ways to use it up! This is loosely based on my Aunt Jeanie's chicken salad.

6-8 oz. cooked chicken-chopped (3-4 oz. per person)
⅓ cup celery-chopped
½ cup *mayonnaise (Phase 1)
½ tsp. salt
⅛ tsp. pepper
1 green onion-green and white parts thinly sliced
2 tsp. red onion (if you don't have red onion, white or yellow will be fine)
½ tsp. *AP seasoning
1 tsp. tarragon (optional)

Mix all ingredients together and serve on a bed of lettuce.

The flavor will be best if it sits for at least a few hours or overnight.

Phase 3: Add some slivered almonds for some extra crunch!

Creamy Crab, Shrimp, or Tuna Salad (Phase 1)

Follow the recipe above, except replace the cooked chicken with 6-8 oz. cooked crab, shrimp, or tuna and omit the tarragon and slivered almonds. Place each serving on a bed of lettuce. Add 2 tomatoes, quartered, and one hard-boiled egg, quartered, divide among the two salads and serve!

Black Bean Salad (Phase 2)

1 cup cooked black beans

1 cup *Italian-style dressing

½ green bell pepper — cut into small dice

1 avocado — cut into small dice

1 large tomato — cut into small dice

2 tbsp. red onion — minced

2 tbsp. green onion — thinly sliced

¼ cup fresh cilantro — minced

½ tsp. chili powder

⅛ tsp. garlic powder

1 tsp. cumin

⅛ tsp. pepper

Combine all ingredients and let sit, refrigerated, for at least 4-6 hours before serving for the best flavor.

Phase 3: Add ½ cup whole kernel corn (fresh- cooked or frozen and defrosted) and 2 tsp. fresh lime juice.

Coleslaw (Phase 1)

¾ cup *mayonnaise

¾ cup Greek yogurt

2 tbsp. xylitol

1 tsp. salt

⅛ tsp. garlic powder

⅛ tsp. *celery salt

1 pinch of paprika

1 head cabbage (medium size) — thinly sliced

1 large carrot, top and bottom removed — shredded

Combine all ingredients except cabbage and carrot in a bowl. Add cabbage and carrot and stir to combine. Cover with a tight-fitting lid or plastic wrap. This will be best if you let it sit covered in the refrigerator for at least 4 hours. Toss again before serving.

Fajita Salad (Phase 1)

2 tsp. + 1 tsp. *AP seasoning

1 Lb. flank steak, skirt steak, or chicken — cut across the grain into thin strips

2 tsp. + 1 tsp. cumin

2 tbsp. oil

1 bell pepper — cut into thin strips

1 onion — cut into thin strips

1 large clove garlic — minced or pressed

1 cup *tomato salsa

½ cup Greek yogurt

6 cups lettuce-torn into bite-sized pieces

*Italian-style dressing

Rub the meat with 2 tsp. each of the *AP seasoning and cumin and refrigerate for half an hour.

Heat 1 tbsp. of the oil on medium-high and add the peppers, onion, remaining *AP seasoning, and cumin, and cook for about 3-5 minutes until crisp-tender. Remove veggies from the pan and set aside.

Add remaining 1 tbsp. oil to the pan and cook the meat for about 3 minutes or until the doneness you prefer. Add the veggies back to the pan and stir.

To serve, toss the lettuce with just enough of the *Italian-style dressing to lightly coat the salad and divide onto 4 plates. Top each with ¼ of the meat mixture, and top that with the *salsa and yogurt. Enjoy!

Cucumber Yogurt Salad (Phase 1)

This is loosely based on my Aunt Cleo's cucumber salad.

½ cup plain Greek yogurt
½ tsp. salt + more for sprinkling (see below)
¼ tsp. dill weed
2 medium cucumbers or 1 English cucumber — very thinly sliced (this is a good place to use a mandolin; a Japanese one is about $20)

Place cucumber slices in a single layer in a colander and liberally salt them. Repeat layers of cucumber and salt. Let sit for 60 minutes. Rinse off all the salt and pat dry.

Combine all the other ingredients (except the cucumber). Add the cucumber and mix well. Refrigerate in an airtight container for at least 4 hours for the best flavor.

Chef Salad (Phase 2)

2 cups lettuce-torn into bite-sized pieces

1 oz. Colby cheese-cut into ½" x ½" slices

1 oz. jack cheese-cut into ½" x ½" slices

2 oz. home-cooked chicken (like left over *mock beer can chicken) or turkey-diced

1 medium tomato-diced (or 6 cherry tomatoes-halved)

½ avocado-diced

1 hard-boiled egg-diced

2-3 tbsp. *ranch-style dressing or *Italian-style dressing

You may lay out the lettuce and arrange all of the other ingredients on top and serve the dressing on the side. Or, you may toss all of the ingredients together for a more casual style.

Macaroni Salad (Phase 2)

1 cup uncooked brown rice pasta (macaroni, elbow macaroni, small shells, or fusilli)
½ cup *mayonnaise
1 tbsp. onion — finely chopped
1½ tbsp. celery — finely chopped
½ tsp. *AP seasoning
¼ tsp. pepper
¾ cup salad shrimp
½ cup peas — thawed, if frozen

Cook pasta according to package directions, adding 1-2 tbsp. salt to the water once it boils. Drain and rinse under cold water in a colander. Let cool before adding other ingredients or the *mayonnaise will melt. Mix macaroni with other ingredients, cover, and refrigerate for one hour or overnight to meld the flavors together.

Tip: You may replace the shrimp with cooked chicken and add ½ tsp. dried thyme or tarragon.

Pasta Salad (Phase 2)

(Pictured on Cover)

2 cups raw or blanched broccoli (even leftover cooked broccoli would work)

½ cup *Italian-style dressing

½ cup peas-blanched (or thawed, if frozen)

2 green onions-finely chopped

1 tbsp. finely chopped red onion (if you don't have red, white or yellow will do)

2 carrots-diced

½ pint cherry tomatoes-halved

3 cups cooked, rinsed, and cooled brown rice pasta (you need to rinse this and let this cool or it will absorb too much dressing and become gummy)

Combine all ingredients and let sit, refrigerated, for several hours or overnight. The flavor will continue to improve the longer it sits.

Note: Feel free to use any shape of pasta you like. The medium type (farfale, elbow macaroni, fusilli, and penne) work best.

Tip: For a heartier version, you can toss in some cooked chicken, tuna, or turkey.

Phase 3: Add ½ cup each: green beans, kidney beans, garbanzo beans, and corn, and ⅓ cup grated Parmesan cheese.

Shrimp or Crab Green Salad (Phase 1)

8 cups lettuce

16 oz. cooked shrimp or crab

4 tomatoes-quartered

4 hard-boiled eggs-quartered

½ cup carrot-shredded

1 green onion-finely sliced

½ cup celery-diced

*dressing of your choice

Divide the lettuce among the 4 plates. Mound the shrimp or crab in the center of the plate and alternate the egg and tomato wedges around the outer edge of each plate. Sprinkle the carrot, onion and celery over the top of the salad and drizzle the *dressing over all, and serve.

Phase 2: Dice 1 avocado and sprinkle on the salad for more color and flavor.

Taco Salad (Phase 1)

1 Lb. ground beef, chicken, or turkey

1 small onion-diced

1 large clove garlic-minced or pressed

½ bell pepper-diced

1 tbsp. *AP seasoning

1 tbsp. cumin

6 cups lettuce-torn into bite-sized pieces

1 large tomato-diced

1 green onion-finely chopped

*Italian-style dressing (to taste)

Brown the meat in a skillet. Drain off the excess fat and add the onion, garlic, bell pepper, *AP seasoning, and cumin. Cook for 10-15 minutes until the onion and bell pepper are soft.

Let mixture cool or cover and refrigerate until ready to use.

Toss the meat mixture with the lettuce, tomato, green onion, and enough *Italian-style dressing to lightly coat the salad and serve.

Phase 2: Add 1 large avocado (cubed) and ½ cup of shredded Colby cheese.

Chicken Caesar Salad (Phase 3)

1 large head of romaine lettuce-torn into bite-sized pieces
2 cups home cooked chicken-cut or torn into bite-sized pieces
*Caesar salad dressing
1/3 cup Parmesan cheese-shredded

Toss lettuce and chicken with enough *Caesar salad dressing to lightly coat the salad. Sprinkle the Parmesan on top and serve.

Tip: You may add *sliced almond snacks for the crunch that's missing from the croutons.

Soups & Stews

Beef Pot Roast (Phase 1)

I suggest using chuck roast here, but the following will also work for this pot roast: top or bottom round, brisket, blade, rump, or shoulder. This recipe can be cooked either on the stove in a Dutch oven, in the oven in a Dutch oven (with a lid and handles that are oven-safe), or in a slow cooker (which I prefer).

2 tsp. oil
3-4 Lb. beef roast (see choices above)
2 tsp. *AP seasoning
1 tbsp. *tomato paste
1 medium onion-diced
1 carrot-diced
1 rib celery-diced
1 large clove garlic-smashed or roughly chopped
½ bell pepper-diced
1 large or 2 small-medium *whole peeled tomatoes
½ cup *chicken stock
1 cup water
1 tsp. dried thyme
1 tsp. dried basil
½ tsp. dried oregano

Heat oil in a Dutch oven if you're going to cook it in the oven, on the stove (see note above), or in any pan that will hold the roast alone if cooking in a slow cooker. Season the meat on all sides with the *AP Seasoning. Brown meat in the oil on all sides and add to the slow cooker, or leave in the Dutch oven if using. Add the *tomato paste and sauté for about 3–5 minutes.

Add the rest of the ingredients to the meat and cover.
If using a Crock-Pot, set on low for 8-9 hours or on high for 3½ to 4½ hours. If using a Dutch oven, cook on low heat on the stove, or at 325° in the oven, for 3½ to 4½ hours or until meat is very tender. If the liquid level goes below the meat while cooking, you may need to add additional water to cover.

Phase 4: Replace ½ cup of *chicken stock with 1 cup of red wine or beer.

Beef Stew (Phase 1)

2 tbsp. oil

1½-2 Lb. beef chuck-cubed (or any stew meat you choose)

¾ tsp. *AP seasoning

2 carrots-chopped

2 stalks celery-chopped

1 onion-chopped

1 tbsp. *tomato paste

6 cups water (+ up to 2 cups water, if needed)

1 medium zucchini-chopped

2 or 3 large *whole peeled tomatoes

1 large clove garlic-minced or pressed

½ tsp. salt

¼ tsp. pepper

1 tsp. each, dried: thyme, basil, parsley, and oregano

Heat oil in a Dutch oven on medium-high until fragrant. Season beef with *AP seasoning. Brown meat on all sides and remove from pan. Add carrots, celery, onion, and *tomato paste and sauté for about 5 minutes. Add 6 cups of water and the balance of ingredients (reserving the 2 cups of water until needed) and bring to a boil. Cover and reduce heat to simmer for 30-40 minutes.

Remove 3 cups of soup liquid and some of the veggies to a blender and blend until smooth; this will help thicken the stew somewhat.

Add back to the pot with the beef and cook on medium, uncovered, for 2 – 2½ hours until meat is tender (add more water if stew gets too thick or if the liquid level falls below the meat). Adjust seasoning to taste.

<u>Phase 2</u>: Add 2 bay leaves with the other herbs. Before browning meat, toss it in a bag with ¾ – 1 cup brown rice flour seasoned with ¾ tsp. *AP seasoning. Remove the meat to the pot of hot oil and continue as above. Instead of blending 3 cups of veggies and liquid as above, you may make a slurry of 1½ tbsp. of the flour left in the bag with ½ cup of the soup liquid from the pot — shake together in a container with a tight-fitting lid until there are no lumps. Add this slurry to the pot, just before you add the meat back in, and stir in thoroughly. Bring to a boil, stirring occasionally. Reduce heat to simmer and continue as above.

Chicken Veggie Soup (Phase 1)

(Pictured on Opposite Page)

2 quarts *chicken stock

2 carrots-chopped

2 ribs of celery-chopped

¾ cup onion-chopped

2 cups zucchini-chopped

2 cups *whole peeled tomatoes-chopped

1 tsp. salt

½ tsp. pepper

½ tsp. *AP seasoning

2 cups chicken-cooked and torn or cubed into bite-sized pieces

Bring the *chicken stock to a boil, then reduce heat to a simmer. Add all other ingredients except chicken and cook for 10-15 minutes until green beans are crisp-tender.

Add chicken and simmer for another 5 minutes to warm it through.

Phase 2: Add 2 cups cooked brown rice pasta, cooked and cubed potatoes, or cooked brown rice, if desired.

Phase 3: Add 1 cup green beans cut into bite-sized pieces and sprinkle a little Parmesan cheese on top.

Chicken Stock (Phase 1)

I like to save the chicken necks and carcasses from 2-3 of my *mock beer can chickens, in the freezer, and use them to make this stock. Any chicken bones will work.

2 Lb. chicken bones, with or without meat, raw or cooked
3 whole carrots — cut in half
3 celery ribs (including leaves) — cut in half
2 medium onions — cut in half
2–3 sprigs thyme
10 whole peppercorns
1 tbsp. salt
3 stalks fresh parsley
4 quarts water

Place all ingredients into a large stock pot. Bring water almost to a boil, then reduce to a simmer (skim the scum from the top as needed). Continue to simmer for 4–6 hours, then strain through a cheesecloth-lined strainer or colander.

Tip: I like to store this in small airtight containers in the freezer or make these into ice cubes and store them in zip-top freezer bags.

Veggie Stock (Phase 1)

6 carrots

6 stalks celery

1 large onion — cut in half

4–6 medium tomatoes (optional)

1 leek — sliced down the middle lengthwise and washed well (leeks can be very dirty!)

3 large cloves garlic

6 sprigs fresh parsley

3 sprigs fresh thyme

1 tbsp. salt

6 quarts filtered water

Place all ingredients into a large stock pot. Bring to a boil, then reduce to a simmer. Continue to cook for 1 ½ – 2 hours then strain through a cheesecloth lined strainer or colander.

Tip: I like to store this in small airtight containers in the freezer or make these into ice cubes and store them in freezer bags in the freezer.

Phase 2: Add 3 bay leaves.

Gazpacho (Phase 1)

(Pictured on Opposite Page)

½ tsp. *AP seasoning

2 medium tomatoes-chopped (reserving 2 tsp.-minced)

¼ cup green bell pepper-chopped (reserving 2 tsp.-minced)

¼ cup cucumber-seeded and chopped (reserving 2 tsp.-minced)

1 tbsp. oil

1 clove of garlic

1 green onion-chopped (reserving 2 tsp.-minced)

½ tsp. jalapeno-seeded, deveined, and chopped

1 tsp. anchovy paste

½ tsp. salt

¼ tsp. pepper

3 tbsp. chopped cilantro (reserving 2 tsp.minced)

Place all ingredients (except the reserved quantities) into a blender or food processor. Blend thoroughly (pulse for a chunky version). Cover and refrigerate 4-6 hours or longer. Place the soup in bowls and sprinkle with 2 tsp. each: tomato, bell pepper, cucumber, green onion and cilantro (all minced) on top of the chilled soup and serve.

Phase 2: Replace the AP seasoning with taco seasoning.

Phase 4: Add 1 tablespoon red wine vinegar and replace the jalapeno with ¼ teaspoon hot sauce.

Manhattan Clam Chowder (Phase 1)

2 tsp. oil

1 large clove of garlic-minced or pressed

½ cup onion-diced

¼ cup celery-diced

½ tsp. salt

¼ tsp. pepper

½ cup *whole peeled tomatoes with juice-chopped

2 cups clam juice

½ tsp. dried thyme

18 small fresh clams-well scrubbed (or 1 6.5-oz. can chopped clams, *no sugar added!*)

Heat oil in a soup pot and sauté garlic, onion, celery, salt, and pepper for 5-10 minutes. Add tomatoes, clam juice, and thyme. Simmer for 15-20 minutes. Add clams, cover, and simmer for another 10 minutes or until the clams are all open. Remove the clams from the shell, chop, and add back to the soup. Make sure to discard any clams that don't open.

Lentil Soup (Phase 3)

2 tsp. olive oil

½ cup onion-finely diced or shredded

½ cup celery-finely diced or shredded

½ cup carrot-finely diced or shredded

1 clove garlic-roughly chopped

1 tbsp. *AP seasoning

1 bay leaf

16 oz. dried lentils-sorted, rinsed, and drained

6 cups *chicken stock or *vegetable stock (or more, so lentils are covered and wet through cooking)

¼ cup prosciutto-finely diced (or 2 sausage links, sliced ½" thick)

Heat oil in a soup pot on medium-high and sauté everything but the lentils, *stock, and prosciutto or sausage for 5-10 minutes until softened. Add the remaining ingredients and stir to combine. Reduce heat, cover, and simmer for 1½-2 hours or until lentils are tender but not mushy. Adjust seasoning to taste.

Tip: Sprinkle 1 teaspoon of Parmesan cheese on top of each serving.

Cream of Broccoli Soup (Phase 2)

(Pictured on Opposite Page)

2 cups broccoli-roughly chopped
1½ cups *chicken stock or *veggie stock
½ cup chopped onion
1 bay leaf
1 tsp. *AP seasoning
1 pinch celery salt
½ tsp. salt
¼ tsp. pepper
⅛ tsp. nutmeg
2 tbsp. butter
2 tbsp. brown rice flour
1 cup rice milk

Place the first 9 ingredients in a saucepan and bring to a boil. Reduce heat, cover, and simmer for 10 minutes or until the broccoli is tender.

Discard the bay leaf, then process the mixture in a blender or food processor for 1-2 minutes and set aside. Process in 2 batches so it won't explode from the steam.

In the same saucepan, melt the butter and flour and whisk for about 1 minute. Add the milk all at once and continue stirring until the mixture thickens. Add the broccoli liquid back to the pot and heat through. Season to taste, and top each bowl with a dollop of yogurt if desired.

Phase 3: Sprinkle each bowl with 1 teaspoon Parmesan cheese.

Main Dishes

Beef Stroganoff (Phase 2)

1 large onion — sliced

4 tbsp. butter

¾ tsp. *AP seasoning

2 Lb. London broil — sliced into thin 3" strips

½ cup brown rice flour

1 tbsp. *fresh grated horseradish (*don't use the jarred version*)

¼ – ⅛ tsp. red pepper flakes (or more, depending on how spicy you like it)

¾ cup water

¾ cup plain Greek yogurt

Sauté onion in butter on medium heat, until soft but without color (about 5 minutes). Set aside.

Season meat with *AP seasoning and toss into brown rice flour. Brown meat on both sides, then dot with *horseradish and hot pepper flakes. Add water, cover, and simmer on low heat for 3 hours. Stir in yogurt and serve over cooked spaghetti squash, cooked brown rice, or brown rice pasta noodles.

Phase 4: Replace the hot pepper flakes with 1 tbsp. *chili sauce. Sauté ¾ cup of sliced mushrooms with the onions, then continue as above.

Asian-Style Beef (Phase 2)

I really struggled to find an Asian-inspired dish without using soy sauce or any other fermented Asian sauces. While this would be better with soy sauce, I think it's pretty good for what is allowed.

1 tbsp. + 1 tbsp. oil

4–5 cloves garlic-finely minced or pressed

3 tbsp. fresh ginger-finely minced or grated

1 tsp + 2 tsp. toasted sesame oil

4 green onions-finely sliced

3 tbsp. cilantro leaves-roughly chopped

1 Lb. beef-thinly sliced into 1" strips

1 bell pepper-chopped

½ Lb. broccoli florets-blanched for 3-5 minutes

1 large carrot-diced and blanched for 3-5 minutes

1 tsp. *AP seasoning

¾ cup peas-defrosted, if frozen

Place 1 tablespoon oil, garlic, ginger, 1 teaspoon sesame oil, half the green onion, half the cilantro, and meat into a zip top bag. Marinate for 6-8 hours.

Heat 1 tablespoon oil in a large sauté pan. Remove meat from marinade and sauté for 2–3 minutes per side. Remove from pan and set aside. Add broccoli, carrot, *AP seasoning, and peas to the pan and sauté for 5 minutes. Add back the meat and the rest of the green onion, then add 2 teaspoons sesame oil and the rest of the cilantro, toss all together, and serve on a bed of brown rice.

Tip: You may substitute chicken, shrimp, or organic, firm tofu (cubed) for the beef.

Phase 4: Add 2 teaspoons soy sauce to the marinade, and 2 more teaspoons with the addition of the meat. The soy sauce is salty, so you may have to adjust the seasoning for this.

Stuffed Bell Peppers (Phase 1)

4 large bell peppers

1 Lb. ground beef (ground turkey or ground chicken may be substituted)

½ cup onion — diced

2 tbsp. *AP seasoning

1 tsp. dried thyme

1 large clove garlic — minced or pressed

½ cup cooked brown rice

½ cup *whole peeled tomatoes

Preheat oven to 350°. Cut tops off peppers, remove seeds and membranes, and reserve tops. Cook beef and drain off excess oil. Add onion, *AP seasoning, thyme, garlic, rice, and tomatoes and mix well. Lightly stuff peppers and replace tops. Stand the peppers up in an 8" x 8" baking dish and bake for 45 minutes.

Tip: Serve with warmed *tomato sauce on top or put the sauce on the peppers before adding the tops so the sauce cooks into the meat mixture.

Phase 2: Add one half cup Colby cheese to the meat mixture.

Broiled Fish Filet (Phase 1)

1 firm fish filet, 1" thick (swordfish, salmon, halibut, red snapper, cod, sea bass, etc.)

1 tbsp. butter — melted

$\frac{1}{8}$ tsp. dill weed

$\frac{1}{4}$ tsp. *AP seasoning

Preheat broiler to high.

Place fish on a rack over a pan that can go under the broiler.

Mix together the butter, dill, and *AP seasoning.

Spread half of the butter mixture on the top side of the fish.

Place rack 3–4 inches from the heat source.

Place the fish under the broiler for 7–8 minutes. Flip over and paint with the other half of the butter mixture. Broil for another 5–8 minutes or until fish is firm but not overcooked.

Tip: Serve with *tartar sauce (Phase 1) and *coleslaw!

Phase 2: Serve salmon with *Hollandaise sauce.

Phase 3: Add $\frac{1}{4}$ teaspoon of lemon zest to the butter mixture. Squeeze fresh lemon juice over the cooked fish and serve with *tartar sauce.

Poor Man's Scallone (Phase 1)

(Pictured on Opposite Page)

2 sea scallops

1 calamari steak or ¼ Lb. whole — cleaned

1 egg

½ tsp. *AP seasoning

1 tbsp. oil

Place all ingredients, except the oil, in a food processor or blender and purée until fully ground (it will be a paste).

Heat the oil on medium heat in an 8" nonstick pan. Pour the mixture in the pan and spread it to an even thickness. Brown on both sides (about 3 minutes per side). The mixture will firm up to resemble a cooked abalone steak.

Serve with Phase 1 *tartar sauce.

Phase 3: Squeeze a little lemon juice on top of the fish before serving and with *tartar sauce on the side (optional).

Chicken and Pesto Pasta (Phase 3)

2 cups brown rice pasta (fusilli, farfale, penne, or similarly sized and shaped pasta)

1 cup *pesto sauce

1 cup cooked broccoli or peas (if frozen, thawed)

1½ cups cooked chicken—cubed or torn into bite-sized pieces

¼ cup Parmesan cheese—grated

Cook and drain pasta and place in a large bowl. Toss with the *pesto sauce until well mixed. Add the veggies, chicken, and Parmesan, and toss to combine.

Tip: This is a great way to use up leftover *mock beer can chicken.

Fajitas (Phase 2)

1 Lb. beef flank steak, skirt steak, or chicken

2 tsp. + 1 tsp. *taco seasoning

6-8 *corn tortillas

2 tbsp. oil

1 bell pepper-sliced into thin strips

1 onion-sliced into thin strips

1 cup *tomato salsa

½ cup Greek yogurt (optional)

1 cup *guacamole or avocado slices (optional)

Rub 2 teaspoons *taco seasoning on the meat and refrigerate for at least half an hour, up to 8 hours.

Cut the meat into thin strips (being sure to cut across the grain).

Heat the *corn tortillas (wrapped in foil to prevent them from drying out) in a 200° oven until warm.

Place 1 tablespoon of the oil in a skillet heated to medium-high. Add peppers, onion, and remaining 1 teaspoon of the *taco seasoning. Sauté for about 3-5 minutes until crisp-tender. Remove veggies from the pan and add the remaining 1 tablespoon of the oil, and sauté the meat for about 3 minutes or until cooked to the doneness you prefer. Add the veggies back to the pan and toss together.

To serve, place the meat and veggie mixture in a warmed *corn tortilla and top with *tomato salsa, a dollop of Greek yogurt, and *guacamole or avocado slices.

Note: If you're in Phase 1 and craving fajitas, you can make *fajita salad or wrap in a *mock tortilla!

Cheese-Stuffed Chicken Breasts or Thighs (Phase 2)

(Pictured on Opposite Page)

1 chicken breast or 2 thighs—bone in, skin on
1 tbsp. each: Colby and Jack cheese (or any cheese you're allowed)
2 tsp. green onion—finely minced
½ tsp. olive oil
⅛ tsp. *AP seasoning

Preheat oven to 375°.

Combine all ingredients except chicken and oil. Lift the skin of the chicken and stuff the filling between the chicken skin and meat. Pull the skin back over the filling, rub the skin with the oil, and sprinkle the *AP seasoning evenly over the top.

Bake for 45–50 minutes or until the breast reads 170° or the thighs read 180° on an instant read thermometer.

Tip: For a southwestern flavor, you may substitute the *AP seasoning with *taco seasoning and add 2 teaspoons *roasted, green chiles to the filling mixture.

Stuffed Zucchini (Phase 2)

1 Lb. ground beef, lamb, turkey, or chicken

1 small onion-diced

2 cloves garlic-minced or pressed

1 bell pepper-diced

1 cup *whole peeled tomatoes

1 tsp. dried basil

3 tbsp. *AP seasoning

1½ cups brown rice-cooked

1 jumbo (or 6 medium) zucchini

½ cup Colby cheese

Preheat oven to 350°. Sauté meat until browned, drain off excess fat, then add the onion, garlic, bell pepper, *whole peeled tomatoes, and basil and cook until veggies are softened (about 10 minutes). Add *AP seasoning, rice and cheese, then stir to combine.

Cut zucchini in half lengthwise and scoop out the center, leaving a ¾" rim around the entire jumbo zucchini, or scoop out all of the seeds in the medium zucchini if using. Divide the filling evenly into the zucchini halves. Cover with foil and bake for 20-30 minutes until zucchini is cooked.

Tip: You may cook this (wrapped in foil) on the grill.

Phase 3: You may replace Colby cheese with cheddar or Parmesan cheese.

Lasagna (Phase 1)

1 recipe of *meat sauce for pasta
4 *mock tortillas cut into strips (or you may use thinly sliced and grilled eggplant or zucchini cut lengthwise, cabbage leaves with ribs removed, or any other allowed veggie, thinly sliced and blanched)

Preheat oven to 350°. Spread a small amount of sauce on the bottom of a 9" x 13" baking pan. Place one layer of *mock tortilla strips (or veggie slices) on the bottom of the pan, over sauce. Alternate layers of sauce and *mock tortillas (or veggie slices), ending with a thin layer of sauce on top. Bake for 1 hour. Let cool 15 minutes before slicing.

Phase 2: Replace *mock tortillas with brown rice lasagna noodles or thinly sliced organic extra firm tofu. Add 1 16-ounce container of ricotta cheese (layered under the sauce) and 6-8 ounces of both shredded Colby and jack cheese (or cheese of your choice allowed in phase 2) over sauce.

Phase 3: Replace the Colby and jack cheeses with mozzarella cheese and ½ cup Parmesan cheese sprinkled on top. This will have a much stronger, more authentic lasagna flavor.

Chicken or Beef Enchiladas (Phase 1)

(Pictured on Opposite Page with Refried Beans and Mexican Style Rice)

4 *mock tortillas

1½ cups cooked chicken, cooked ground beef, cooked or leftover steak

1 green onion—finely chopped

½ tsp. *AP seasoning

1 cup *salsa

1 tbsp. fresh cilantro—finely chopped (+ whole sprigs for garnish-optional)

Preheat oven to 350°. Divide the meat, onion, and *AP seasoning evenly into the *mock tortillas. Place them, seam side down, in an 8" x 8" casserole dish, cover with the *salsa, and bake for 30 minutes. Serve with a dollop of yogurt and a sprig of cilantro.

Tip: This is another great place to use leftover *mock beer can chicken!

Tip 2: For a spicier version, you may add minced jalapeño with the meat and spices.

Phase 2: You may replace the *mock tortillas with *corn tortillas that have been heated and wrapped in foil, in a 200° oven for 5 minutes to soften them. You may add a pinch of *taco seasoning and two tablespoon each, Jack and Colby cheese and add sliced, *roasted green chiles. Serve with avocado slices on top.

Meat Sauce for Pasta (and so much more!) (Phase 1)

(Pictured on Scrambled Eggs)

1 Lb. ground beef, turkey, or chicken

2 tsp. oil

½ medium onion—diced

1 small bell pepper-diced

1½ tsp. *AP seasoning

2 cloves garlic—finely minced or pressed

1 tbsp. *tomato paste

2 cups water

1½ cups *tomato sauce

2 tsp. basil

2 tsp. thyme

2 tsp. oregano

2 cups *whole peeled tomatoes

4 oz. *homemade breakfast sausage—cooked and crumbled

Brown ground beef in a Dutch oven on medium-high. Drain off excess fat and set meat aside. In the same pot, reduce heat to medium, add the oil, and sauté the onion, bell pepper, and *AP seasoning until the onions are translucent (about 5 minutes). Add garlic and *tomato paste and sauté another 2-3 minutes. Add water, *tomato sauce, all the herbs, *whole peeled tomatoes, *homemade breakfast sausage, and ground beef, and stir until well incorporated.

Reduce heat to low and let cook on a low simmer for at least 2-3 hours. Adjust seasoning to taste. The longer you simmer this the better it will taste.

Tip: I suggest you make a double or triple batch of this, as it's really versatile. You can use it on scrambled eggs with a dollop of yogurt and minced chives, in lasagna, or with any pasta you like.

Tip 2: To make a non-meat version, follow the same recipe but leave out the meat. It will still make a great tomato flavored pasta sauce.

Phase 2: Add 2 bay leaves for a richer flavor.

Phase 3: Sprinkle Parmesan cheese on top of each serving.

Phase 4: Add one half cup dry red wine and 6–8 sliced mushrooms for the best flavor.

Moussaka (Phase 2)

This recipe has a lot of steps, but it's well worth it!

2 Lb. eggplant—peeled & sliced ½" thick

1 Lb. ground beef, lamb, or ½ Lb. of each

1 cup onion—chopped

¼ cup water

2 tbsp. parsley

1 tbsp. *tomato paste

1 tsp. salt + more to sprinkle on eggplant slices

½ tsp. pepper

⅓ cup cooked brown rice

½ cup Colby cheese—shredded

2 + 1 egg(s)—beaten

¼ tsp. ground cinnamon

3 tbsp. butter

3 tbsp. brown rice flour

½ tsp. *AP seasoning

⅛ tsp. nutmeg

1½ cups rice milk

Sprinkle eggplant slices with salt and set in a colander in the sink to drain off their bitter juices. After 30 minutes, rinse off the salt and pat them dry.

Preheat oven to 350°. Cook meat and onion in a skillet, on medium-high, until browned; drain off excess fat.

Stir in water, parsley, *tomato paste, salt, and pepper. Simmer until liquid is almost completely evaporated (about 3-5 minutes). Set aside to cool slightly.

Stir the rice, half the cheese, 2 eggs, and cinnamon into the meat mixture. Set aside.

Melt butter in a saucepan and whisk in the flour, *AP seasoning, and nutmeg. Add the rice milk all at once, whisking until thick and bubbly.

Stir half the sauce mixture into the beaten egg and return all to the saucepan, stirring over low heat for 2 minutes.

Brown eggplant slices either on a grill, grill pan, or in a little oil in a skillet. *Be careful with the oil (if using), as the eggplant will absorb it like a sponge*! Lay half of the eggplant slices in the bottom of a 12" x 7" x 2" baking dish.

Spoon meat mixture over eggplant layer. Place the other half of the eggplant over the mixture and pour the sauce over all.

Sprinkle with remaining cheese.

Bake, uncovered, until set (about 45 minutes).

Tip: Serve this with *ratatouille for a Mediterranean-style dinner.

Phase 4: **Add ¼ cup red wine with the parsley.**

Paella Casserole (Phase 2)

2 tbsp. *AP seasoning

1½ Lb. chicken pieces—bone in, skin on

1 tbsp. olive oil

½ medium onion—diced

½ red bell pepper—diced

½ green bell pepper—diced

2 large cloves garlic—minced or pressed

¾ cup *whole peeled tomatoes—chopped

1 tsp. salt

½ tsp. pepper

2 cups brown rice (or rice of choice)

¼ – ½ tsp. saffron threads

1 cup hot water

2 cups hot *chicken stock

4 oz. *homemade breakfast sausage—cooked and crumbled (or other sausage, not cured or smoked with sugar, cooked and cut into ½" pieces)

½ Lb. prawns—peeled and deveined (thawed if frozen)

¼ cup peas (thawed if frozen)

Lemon wedges for garnish (optional)

Season both sides of the chicken with the *AP seasoning and let marinate in the refrigerator for 1 hour.

Preheat oven to 375°. Heat oil over medium-high heat in a paella pan, or other wide, shallow ovenproof pan. Brown chicken on both sides and remove from pan but reserve the drippings.

Add to the pan the onion, red and green bell pepper, garlic, *whole peeled tomatoes, salt, and pepper and cook until veggies are tender (about 5 minutes).

Add uncooked rice and saffron and stir until the rice is evenly coated with the fat. Add the hot water and hot *chicken stock. Bring mixture to a boil, nestle chicken pieces into the rice, cover, and bake for 30 minutes.

Place *homemade breakfast sausage or (allowed) link slices, prawns, and peas in and around chicken pieces on top of the rice mixture and bake, covered, for another 6-8 minutes until prawns are pink.

Garnish with lemon wedges if desired.

Tip: You may add other seafood (like fresh clams or muscles).

Tip 2: If you'd like your paella spicy, you can add from a pinch to ½ tsp. cayenne pepper or crushed red pepper flakes.

Pork Chops and Scalloped Potatoes (Phase 2)

4 pork chops—sprinkled with ⅛ tsp. salt and pinch of pepper per side, per chop

2 tsp. olive oil

1 cup onion—thinly sliced

2 cloves garlic—minced or pressed

½ cup *mayonnaise

1 ½ cups yogurt

1 tsp. anchovy paste

2 tbsp. chopped parsley

⅛ tsp. *celery salt

1 tsp. salt

½ tsp. pepper

¼ cup *chicken stock

3 cups potatoes—thinly sliced (it's helpful to use a mandolin or the slicing blade of your food processor for this)

Preheat oven to 350°. Brown pork chops in oil on both sides and place in an 8" x 8" baking dish. Sauté the onion and garlic in the drippings for 5 minutes or until soft, and set aside.

Combine all other ingredients, including the onion and garlic, and layer the potatoes with this sauce mixture on top of the pork chops. Bake for 1 hour, covered, then uncover and bake another 20–30 minutes or until potatoes are tender and top is browned.

Note: I know that adding the drippings may sound odd, but it adds flavor, and if you don't the sauce will separate.

Phase 4: Add ½ cup chopped mushrooms and 1 tsp. Worcestershire sauce.

Pork Loin Roulade (Phase 1)

(Pictured on Opposite Page)

1 tbsp. + 1 tbsp. (for the pan sauce) butter

1 tsp. + 2 tsp. oil

2-3 cloves garlic-chopped

1 small onion-diced

½ bell pepper-diced

½ tsp. salt + 1 tsp. for sprinkling on the outside of the pork

¼ tsp. pepper + ½ tsp. more for sprinkling on the outside of the pork

½ tsp. thyme (you may substitute with finely minced rosemary or sage)

¼ cup + ½ cup (for the pan sauce)*chicken stock

⅛ tsp. *AP seasoning

⅛ tsp. *celery salt

1 pork loin (about 2-3 pounds)

Heat the butter and 1 teaspoon of the oil over medium heat. Add the garlic, onions, bell pepper, ½ tsp. salt, ¼ tsp. pepper, thyme, ¼ cup *chicken stock, *AP seasoning, and *celery salt. Sauté about 5 minutes. Reduce heat to low and cook for 10 minutes or until mixture is soft. Cool for 1 hour, then refrigerate until cold.

Preheat oven to 425°. Place the pork loin on a cutting board and remove any visible silver skin. Slice about a third of the way down the length of the loin without cutting all the way through.

Lay it open like a book, and from what is now the middle of the loin, slice the thick side halfway down the length again, without cutting all the way through, until you can lay it out flat in 3 equal thirds. Pound flat if uneven.

Spread cooled onion mixture evenly on the inside of the loin and roll it up to return it to its original shape. Tie it up along the length of the loin with butcher's twine to hold its shape during roasting. Salt and pepper the outside of the loin. Heat the other 2 teaspoons of oil in a pan on medium-high, and when it's hot, add the loin. Brown on all sides, then move the pan to the oven.

Roast for 20 minutes, then reduce heat to 375° and roast until a meat thermometer reads 150° (about 30-35 minutes). This is another place I highly recommend you use an alarmed, digital thermometer with the probe through the middle of the roast. Make sure to place the probe tip in the meat, not the stuffing.

Allow to rest on a cutting board (covered with foil) for 15 minutes before cutting into 1" slices.

To make a pan sauce, pour most of the grease out of the pan and place the pan back on the burner on medium-high heat, add the *chicken stock, scraping up the bits (fond) from the bottom of the pan. Stir occasionally for about 10 minutes or until the *chicken stock has reduced by about half. Add 1 tablespoon of butter and swirl it around in the pan until it has melted into the sauce. Spoon the sauce over the roast slices and enjoy!

Phase 3: Replace the bell pepper with a chopped tart apple like Granny Smith and add ¼ cup (sugar free-organic) apple juice with the *chicken stock.

Phase 4: Add ¼ cup white wine with the apple juice and *chicken stock.

Roast Leg of Lamb (Phase 1)

1 leg of lamb (3-4 pounds)
2 + 1 clove(s) garlic-2 cut into about 10 slivers; 1 finely minced or pressed
¼ cup chopped mint leaves + 10 small, whole leaves
1 tbsp. oil
2½ tsp *AP seasoning
2 tsp. fresh rosemary-finely minced

Preheat oven to 450°. Cut about 10 slits in the lamb (as evenly spaced apart as possible) and insert one sliver of garlic wrapped in one small mint leaf into each slit.

Mix all remaining ingredients and spread the mixture all over the roast. Place the roast on a rack in an uncovered roasting pan or on a sheet pan. Place the lamb in the oven and immediately reduce the temperature to 325°.

Roast for about 25-35 minutes per pound for medium-rare to medium. I highly recommend an alarmed, digital thermometer (about $20) for this recipe. Insert the probe into the very center of the thickest part of the roast and set the alarm for the desired doneness.

Let the roast rest for about 15 minutes before carving. Spoon a little bit of the pan juices over the slices and serve.

Roast Turkey Breast (Phase 1)

1 half turkey breast
1-2 tbsp. *AP seasoning

Preheat oven to 375°. Sprinkle the *AP seasoning on the turkey breast and place on a rack in a small roasting pan. Roast about 20-25 minutes per pound until the internal temperature reaches 165°.

Let it rest for 10 minutes before slicing.

Note: If you'd like to tuck sage leaves under the skin, it will have more of a Thanksgiving turkey flavor.

Chicken or Veal Cutlet (Phase 2)

1½ Lb. boneless, skinless chicken breasts or veal cutlets—pounded to ¼" thick

2 tbsp. + 1 tbsp. butter

½ cup *chicken stock

½ cup brown rice flour

½ tsp. salt

¼ tsp. pepper

2 tbsp. salt-packed capers (*don't use brined capers!*)

Dredge the meat lightly in the flour, patting off the excess. Sauté in the 2 tablespoons of butter about 3-5 minutes until you see meat juices push up to the top side of the meat; turn over and continue to cook about 3-4 minutes longer.

Deglaze the pan with the *chicken stock and season with salt and pepper. Swirl in the tablespoon of butter and pour over meat.

Phase 3: To make this chicken or veal piccata, replace the *chicken stock with ⅓ cup fresh lemon juice.

Phase 4: To make this chicken or veal marsala, replace the *chicken stock with marsala wine and add one-half pound sliced, sautéed mushrooms.

Side Dishes

Creamed Spinach (Phase 1)

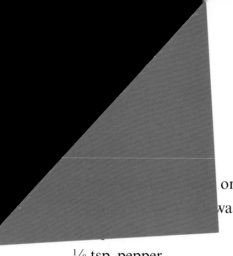

or pressed

washed (or you may use frozen or bagged-fresh spinach)

⅛ tsp. pepper

⅛ tsp. nutmeg

3 tbsp. plain yogurt

½ cup rice or soy milk

Melt butter on medium-high heat. Add garlic and sauté for 2-3 minutes. Add spinach, salt, pepper, and nutmeg and sauté until spinach is limp (about 3 minutes). Add yogurt and rice milk into spinach until heated through. The sauce will become very thick and creamy.

Phase 3: Add ¼ cup Parmesan cheese after adding the rice milk. (If it becomes too thick, just add a little more rice milk.)

Phase 4: Sauté ⅓ cup sliced mushrooms in 2 teaspoons of olive oil, then continue recipe as above.

Gingered Carrots (Phase 1)

1 Lb. carrots-tops and bottoms removed and well scrubbed or peeled

1 tsp. salt

¼ tsp *AP seasoning

1 cup water

2 tbsp. butter

2 tsp. xylitol

1½ tsp. mustard powder

2 tsp. fresh ginger root-peeled and grated

¼ tsp. pepper

¼ tsp. fresh dill-chopped (optional)

Cut the carrots into ¼" crosswise slices (coins). Place 1 teaspoon of salt into boiling water and cook carrots until tender (about 10-12 minutes). Drain off any remaining water and stir in all other ingredients except dill. Continue to cook for an additional 3-5 minutes until the carrots are coated with the sauce. Sprinkle with dill and serve.

Phase 4: Replace xylitol with honey or brown sugar for a more rounded flavor.

Eggplant Casserole (Phase 2)

My dad's aunt (Aunty Stell) used to make a version of this for us every Thanksgiving and Christmas. I substituted the bread with cooked brown rice and I have to say I really like it!

1 eggplant—peeled and cubed

3 tbsp. + 1 tbsp. butter (+ more for buttering the casserole dish)

1 tsp. salt

½ tsp. pepper

1 cup celery-diced

1 tbsp. onion-diced

1 tbsp. parsley-finely chopped or dried

2 eggs-beaten

1 cup brown rice-cooked

Preheat oven to 350°.

Cover eggplant with water and boil until soft (about 10 minutes after it comes to a boil). Drain and mash with a fork or potato masher. Add the 3 tablespoons butter, salt, and pepper and set aside.

Sauté the celery, onion, and parsley in 1 tablespoon of butter for about 5 minutes.

Combine the veggies, rice, eggs and eggplant mixture and pour all into a buttered casserole dish. Bake for 45-50 minutes or until lightly browned on top.

Mexican-Style Rice (Phase 2)

(Pictured with Chicken Enchiladas)

1½ tsp. oil

1½ tbsp. onion or green onion-finely diced

1½ tbsp. bell pepper-finely diced

½ tsp. *taco seasoning

¼ cup *salsa

1 cup cooked brown rice

2 tsp. cilantro-chopped

1 tbsp. Colby cheese-shredded (optional)

Sauté the onion, bell pepper, and *taco seasoning in the oil on medium-high heat for 3-5 minutes until veggies are softened. Add the *salsa and rice and stir for about 2 minutes until heated through. Adjust seasoning to taste. Stir in the cilantro and top with the cheese just before serving.

Phase 3: Add ¼ cup corn kernels (fresh or frozen) with the onion and bell pepper, then continue the recipe as above.

Golden Popovers (Phase 2)

(Pictured on Cover)

Traditionally, popovers are made in a popover pan. I wanted people to be able to make some type of bread without buying specialty equipment so I've adapted the recipe to using a muffin pan. They won't be as tall, but they'll taste just as good!

3 eggs
1 cup brown rice flour
1 cup soy milk
3 tbsp. butter
½ tsp. salt

In a blender or food processor, pulse all ingredients just until blended; don't over beat.
Let rest in refrigerator for at least 1 hour, up to 8 hours.

Preheat oven to 375°. Pour the batter into 8 of the 12 greased, muffin pan cups. Bake for 50 minutes, and make sure you don't open the oven while they're baking. These are best if eaten right away.

<u>Tip:</u> These are a great accompaniment to *rib roast, or to make little sandwiches with turkey, *chicken salad or *creamy shrimp, crab, or tuna salad.

Refried Beans (Phase 3)

(Pictured with Chicken Enchiladas)

1½ cups pinto beans-soaked, cooked, and drained according to package directions
2 tsp. *taco seasoning
2 tsp. olive oil
½ cup water
4 tbsp. *salsa

Heat oil on medium heat and add all ingredients except the salsa. Cook for about 5-8 minutes until the beans are very soft. Mash with a fork or potato masher until competely mashed and creamy (add more water if necessary). Add the salsa and continue to cook until it reaches the texture you desire.

Tip: This is a great side dish to *chicken or beef enchiladas, *fajitas, *taco salad, and *fajita salad.

Italian-Style Zucchini (Phase 1)

4 *whole peeled tomatoes

2 tsp. oil

½ medium onion-diced

2 cloves garlic-minced or pressed

4-5 medium zucchini

1 tsp. dried basil

1½ tsp. dried oregano

½ tsp. salt

¼ tsp. pepper

½ tsp. *AP seasoning

½ cup water

Place tomatoes in a blender, puree, and set aside.

In a saucepan, heat oil on medium-high and sauté the onion and garlic (about 5 minutes).

Add all other ingredients, stir, and reduce heat to medium-low. Simmer, covered, for 15 minutes until zucchini is softened. Uncover and continue to cook until liquid has reduced and thickened (about 5 minutes).

Phase 3: Sprinkle with a little Parmesan cheese on top.

Ratatouille (Phase 1)

1 eggplant-peeled and sliced into ½" slices (about 2½ cups)
2 tbsp. oil
1 medium onion, halved, then thinly sliced (about 1 cup)
1 large green or red bell pepper-seeds and membranes removed, and cut into thin strips
1 tsp. salt + more to sprinkle on eggplant (see below)
½ tsp. pepper
2 cloves garlic
2 medium zucchini-chopped
2 cups *whole peeled tomatoes-chopped
1 tsp. oregano
1 tsp. dried basil
½ tsp. *AP seasoning

Place eggplant slices in a colander and sprinkle with salt. Repeat layers until all the eggplant slices are salted. Let them sit for 30-45 minutes, then rinse the salt off and drain them. Pat them dry, then chop into bite-sized pieces.

Heat oil in a large skillet on medium-high and sauté the onion, bell pepper, salt, and pepper until softened (about 5 minutes). Add remaining ingredients and simmer, covered, over low heat for about 30-45 minutes. Uncover and continue cooking for 15 minutes or until the liquid is reduced to a thick sauce.

Tip: This is a great side dish to *roast leg of lamb and *moussaka.

Phase 3: Sprinkle with a little parmesan cheese on top.

Rice with Veggies (Phase 2)

2 tsp. olive oil

½ medium zucchini-diced

1 small carrot-diced

½ medium onion-diced

1 clove garlic-minced or pressed

1 cup brown rice

1 tsp. salt

¼ tsp. pepper

½ tsp. *AP seasoning

1½ cups *chicken stock

½-1 cup fresh (or frozen, thawed) peas

Heat oil on medium-high heat. Add veggies (except peas) and sauté for 5 minutes. Add rice and toss to evenly coat with oil. Add salt, pepper, *AP seasoning, and the *chicken stock and simmer covered on low heat for 45 minutes. Add peas, stir, and recover. Simmer an additional 5-10 minutes until rice is cooked. Fluff with a fork and serve.

Desserts

Apple Tart (Phase 3)

(Pictured on Opposite Page)

For the filling:

5 cups apples-thinly sliced (I like to use a tart apple like Granny Smith)

½ cup xylitol

1 tsp. ground cinnamon

¼ tsp. nutmeg

⅛ tsp. cloves

½ tsp. salt

2 tsp. lemon juice

1½ tbsp. gluten-free flour (the type doesn't matter here)

Combine all ingredients and set aside.

For the crust:

1 cup butter cut into small cubes and kept very cold

1¼ cups sifted gluten free flour (I use Namaste Perfect Flour Blend)

2 tsp + 2 tsp. xylitol (for sprinkling on the crust)

½ tsp. salt

1 + 1 egg-lightly beaten (keep them separate)

1 tsp. ice water

Cut butter into flour, xylitol, and salt until the size of peas. Combine 1 egg and water, and cut into flour mixture. Don't over-stir (mixture may be crumbly). Place in plastic wrap and refrigerate for 1 hour. Roll out to about ¼" thick (it doesn't need to be a perfect circle).

Place on a parchment-lined sheet pan.

Preheat oven to 425°. Place the apple filling evenly in the center of the dough, leaving a 2" border. Fold the 2" edges of the dough over the apples, pressing gently so they stay in place. Brush the remaining beaten egg over the turned-up edges of the dough and sprinkle with the xylitol.

Bake for 10 minutes, reduce the heat to 350° and bake for an additional 20 minutes or until lightly browned. Let cool for at least 30-60 minutes before serving.

Tip: Don't try to make it perfect. It should be rustic. You want people to know that you cared enough about them to make it yourself!

Zucchini Cake (Phase 3)

1 tbsp. butter (to prepare the pan)

1 cup + 3 tbsp. Namaste flour (to prepare the pan)

1 cup zucchini-shredded

¼ cup xylitol

¼ cup olive oil

2 tbsp. water

½ tsp. salt

½ tsp. nutmeg

½ tsp. cinnamon

½ tsp. cloves

⅔ tsp. baking soda

½ cup pecans or walnuts-chopped

1 egg-lightly beaten

Preheat oven to 350°. Spread an even layer of butter in a loaf pan, then add the 3 tbsp. flour and shake the pan around to evenly coat. Tap out excess flour.

Beat remaining ingredients together with an electric mixer on low speed (about 1 minute). Scrape down the bowl and beat on medium speed for 2 minutes. Pour mixture into the pan and bake for 45 minutes or until a toothpick inserted in the center of the cake comes out clean.

Blueberry Cheesecake (Phase 3)

For the crust:

1½ cups almond meal (without any sugar or anything else added—*check ingredients list*)

4 tbsp. butter-melted

1 tbsp. xylitol

Preheat oven to 350°. Mix all ingredients thoroughly. Press into the bottom and a third of the way up the sides of an 8" or 9" springform pan. Bake for 12 minutes until golden and set aside.

For the filling:

1 cup xylitol

¼ tsp. salt

3 packages cream cheese (8-oz. each)-softened to room temperature

½ cup Greek yogurt

2 tsp. pure vanilla extract

3 eggs

¼ cup cornstarch

1 cup blueberries-thawed, and drained of excess liquid, if frozen

Combine xylitol, salt, cream cheese, yogurt, and vanilla. Mix with an electric mixer until smooth. Add the eggs, one at a time, mixing thoroughly after each addition. Add cornstarch and beat until creamy. Stir in blueberries (by hand) and pour into the pan.

Bake until the top has firmed up (about 50 minutes). If it begins to get brown before it's done, tent it with foil until done. It may still be a little jiggly in the center, but it will firm up as it cools.

Let cool for 1 hour in the oven with the oven door open to avoid cracking. Remove it to the counter until cool. Once at room temperature, put into the refrigerator and chill for at least 2 hours or overnight.

Unlock the pan sides and slice into 8 equal pieces.

Tip: You may serve with a drizzle of *berry syrup on top of each piece.

Tip 2: You don't need to limit yourself to blueberry. The options are limitless—including savory cheesecakes!

Fruit Crisp (Phase 3)

For the fruit:

2 cups chopped fruit (apples, peaches, berries, etc.)

2-4 tbsp. xylitol (depending on how sweet the fruit is)

¼ tsp. salt

½ tsp. pure vanilla extract

½ tsp. cinnamon

⅛ tsp. nutmeg

⅛ tsp. ground cloves (use only if making the apple crisp)

½ tsp. lemon zest

1 tsp. lemon juice

Preheat oven to 375°. Combine all ingredients and divide evenly, into four 4- to 6-ounce ramekins (or you may use a larger one to hold the entire mixture).

For the crisp topping:

½ cup brown rice flour

⅓ cup xylitol

¼ cup butter

½ tsp. salt

½ tsp. cinnamon

1 pinch nutmeg

⅛ tsp. cloves (use only if making the apple crisp)

Combine all ingredients in a food processor or with a fork until crumbly. Spread the crumbly mixture on top of the fruit and bake for 30 minutes until nicely browned on top.

Phase 4: Replace the xylitol with honey or brown sugar for more depth of flavor.

Lemon Soufflé (Phase 3)

(Pictured on Opposite Page)

1-2 tbsp. butter to prepare the soufflé dish

¼ cup xylitol + ¼ cup to prepare the soufflé dish

3 eggs-separated (whites into a *very clean* bowl)

zest of 1 lemon

juice of 1 lemon (about ¼ cup)

Prepare one 8" or four 4-ounce soufflé dishes by buttering the inside, dusting over the butter with the ¼ cup xylitol (it will stick to the butter), and tapping out the excess.

Preheat oven to 350°. Beat the egg yolks until pale (about 2-3 minutes). Add the ⅓ cup xylitol gradually and beat until the eggs are creamy (about 2 minutes). Add the zest and lemon juice, beat for 1 minute, and set aside.

In a *very clean bowl* with *very clean electric beaters*, beat the egg whites until stiff but not dry. If the bowl and beaters aren't free from all fat, the egg whites will not beat up to the volume you need. Fold the whites into the lemon mixture, being careful not to deflate the egg white volume.

(continued on next page)

Pour into the prepared soufflé dish, and place the soufflé dish in a water bath (the water should come about halfway up the side of the dish). Bake for about 35 minutes or until puffed and firm. Serve immediately.

Remember-you wait for the soufflé; it doesn't wait for you!

Tip: If you're making 4 individual soufflés and you don't want to eat them right away, you may freeze them once in the prepared dishes and resume the recipe at the point of the water bath when ready to cook. You do need to realize that, once frozen, they won't puff up as high.

If frozen, you'll have to bake them longer (about 45 minutes or until puffed and firm).

Lemon Yogurt Parfait with Berries (Phase 3)

(Pictured on Cover)

¾ cup plain Greek yogurt

1 tsp. xylitol + more, if fruit is not very sweet

1 tsp. lemon juice

zest of ½ lemon + a pinch for the garnish

⅔-¾ cup berries of your choice + a few for garnish (if using multiple types of berries, keep them seperate)

Mix yogurt, xylitol, lemon juice, and lemon zest and set aside. In a six to eight-ounce parfait dish, place ⅓ of the berries in the bottom, followed by a third of the yogurt mixture, then the raspberries, and top with the rest of the yogurt mixture. Place the garnish berries and pinch of lemon zest on top of the parfait and serve.

Tip: You can eat the lemon yogurt without the berries, too!

Pumpkin Pie (Phase 2)

For the crust:

1 cup butter-cut into small cubes and kept very cold

1¼ cups Namaste Perfect Flour Blend-sifted

2 tsp. xylitol

½ tsp. salt

1 + 1 lightly beaten egg (keep them separate)

1 tsp. ice water

Cut butter into flour, xylitol, and salt until the size of peas. Combine 1 egg and water and cut into flour mixture. Don't over-stir (mixture may be crumbly). Place in plastic wrap in the shape of a disk (for easy rolling later) and refrigerate for at least 1 hour.

Roll out in a circle about ¼" thick (large enough to fill the pie pan, plus an additional ½"-1" all the way around). Place the dough into the pan and tuck the extra ½"-1" border under all the way around, then crimp the edges. Set aside.

For the filling:

15-16 oz. organic pumpkin

1 tbsp. cornstarch

3 large eggs

1 cup soy or rice milk

1½ tsp. vanilla extract

¾ cup xylitol

½ tsp. salt

½ tsp. cinnamon

¼ tsp. ground ginger

pinch of ground cloves

pinch of nutmeg

Preheat oven to 400°. Mix all filling ingredients together and pour into the prepared pan. Brush the remaining beaten egg over the crimped edges of the dough and bake in the middle of the oven for 15 minutes. Reduce the heat to 350° and bake another 45 minutes. Center of filling may still tremble slightly but will continue to set up while it's cooling. Let cool completely before serving.

Vanilla Pudding (Phase 2)

4 egg yolks

2 cups rice milk

$\frac{1}{3}$ cup xylitol

$\frac{1}{8}$ tsp. salt

$\frac{1}{2}$ cup cornstarch

2 tsp. pure vanilla extract

2 tbsp. butter-softened

Place all ingredients except vanilla and butter in a saucepan on medium heat, whisking constantly until thick and bubbly (about 15-20 minutes).

Remove from heat and stir in the vanilla and butter. Pour into individual dishes. If chilling to serve later, place plastic wrap directly on top of pudding to avoid a skin forming.

About the Author

A Purchasing Agent for over 30 years, Diane Bugeia August was diagnosed with Candida Yeast Albicans in 2010. She combined her lifelong love of cooking with her new found passion for creating delicious-to-eat and easy-to-make recipes, that anyone who is diagnosed with this yeast overgrowth can follow.

Her hope is that anyone with Candida, gluten intolerance, or who just want to cut sugar out of their diet, will find her recipes tasting like familiar comfort food that feeds their stomach and their soul!